# HUMAN RIGHTS OF REFUGEES

# Human Rights of Refugees

*(Issues & Concerns in the Globalisation Era)*

**Manish Chaturvedi**

SWASTIK

**SWASTIK PUBLICATIONS**

**DELHI - 110 094 (INDIA)**

HUMAN RIGHTS OF REFUGEES
Issues & Concerns in the Globalisation Era



First Published 2011

ISBN 978-93-80138-68-8



*Published in India by*

SWASTIK PUBLICATIONS
31, Gali No. 1, A-Block, Pocket-5,
CRP Water Tank, Sonia Vihar
Delhi-110094 (INDIA)
email: swastik_books@yahoo.com

---

*Printed at:* Deepak Offset Press, Delhi.

# CONTENTS

# Preface

> "The refugee has been cast adrift, usually because his religion, ethnicity, economic aspirations, political beliefs or political alliances in some way stand opposed to his putative government's efforts to create and sustain a strong nation-state."
>
> —*Rogers Smith*

Refugee problem is a global phenomenon infesting all nations—developed or developing. Refugees are unprotected persons, not just in the sense that their basic liberties or entitlements are in jeopardy, but more fundamentally because it is impossible for them to work within or even to restructure the national community, of which they are nominally a part in order to exercise those human rights. Their position within the home community is not just precarious; there is also an element of fundamental marginalization which distinguishes them from other persons at risk of serious harm.

In the present endeavour we have made an attempt to portray the real picture of refugee problem, its magnitude, and impact on socio-political and economic world order in the era of globalization. Relevant national/international instruments for protecting basic human rights of refugees are also given. The following chapters make core of the study—Introduction; Criteria for Claiming Refugee Status; Regional Instruments; Statelessness; Asylum for Refugees; Refugee Problem: A Socio-political Analysis; Humanitarian

Assistance for Refugees; Ceassation of Refugee Status; Indian Policy on Refugee; Conclusion; Appendices & Bibliography etc.

Definitely, this will serve the purpose of social scientists, social and human rights activists, NGOs and national/ international agencies concerned with the cause of refugees.

This work is substantially based on the information gathered from various official reports of different agencies, and organizations, articles, papers and monographs, prepared by various experts in the field. We owe a deep sense of gratitude to them all. We express our greatfulness to our colleagues, friends and all those who have rendered all assistance and guidance while working on this project. Finally, we are thankful to our publishers for producing this work in nice way.

—MC

# 1

# INTRODUCTION

> "Life affords no higher pleasure than that of surmounting difficulties, passing from one step of success to another, forming new wishes and seeing them gratified. He that labors in any great or laudable undertaking has his fatigues first supported by hope and afterward rewarded by joy."
>
> —*Dr. Samuel Johnson*

In the modern world fierce competition for survival, terrorism, racial-religious conflicts, inter-state warfare, natural calamities and forced occupation of regions by powerful have led to mass exodus of population from their roots to alien adjacent or far-off places. The cause of this may be social, economic or political. Thus emerge the problem of refugees.

Though taking/seeking asylum in a foreign land has had a long history, in the present time many countries of the world are facing the problem of refugee influx. China's occupation of Tibet forced Tibetans to take asylum in India. Similarly Soviet and later US attack on Afghanistan resulted in influx of Afghanis to neighbouring countries. Internal conflict in Sri Lanka caused Tamil mass exodus to India.

Liberation war in Bangladesh gave substantial Bangladeshi refugees to India. Even Muslim terrorism in

Jammu and Kashmir state of India forced Kashmiri Pandits to evacuate the valley (a case of internal displacement).

Such numerous instances of refugee problem are there in other parts of the world.

The problem of the status of refugees dates back to the close of the First World War. The great change in the Political and Social structure in Europe, which particularly followed in the wake of the breakdown of the Centuries-old Russian and Turkish empires, resulted in a mass exodus of persons who were refugees from the new regimes. They were mostly Russians and Armenians, whose total figures amounted to a million persons.

The later establishment of the Fascist regime in Italy resulted in tens of thousands of Italian refugees while the Civil War in Spain added hundreds of thousands of Spanish refugees. The creation of the Nazi regime in Germany and the occupation by Nazi Germany of other regions-resulted in a new wave of refugees.

After the World War II, millions of refugees from East European States sought asylum in western countries, and in the sixties, the new States in Africa had to deal with refugee problems of enormous proportions. In Latin America the flow of persecutes has increased because of political instability in the region.

Refugee status is defined in various international instruments relating to refugees. The early international instruments adopted between the two world wars defined refugees by categories, according to their national or ethnic origin. The various instruments adopted after the Second World War contain general definitions of the term 'refugee'. Refugee status is also defined in regional instruments relating to refugees. Finally, a definition of -refugee status is also contained in the constitution or in the ordinary legislation of a number of countries. However, the authority called upon to apply or implement a legal instrument relating to refugee cannot do so unless the refugees are identified as such.

A man's status as a refugee is determined first and foremost by the factors which led to his condition: expatriation and the breaking of the ties that bound him to the States of his nationality.' A refugee is distinguished from an ordinary alien because of the lack of normalcy of relationship between him and the authorities of his State of origin, arising from the fear of political persecution upon his return. Again, he is distinguished from an ordinary migrant because the reason for his leaving his country is political conditions. An ordinary migrant, or an economic migrant, as distinguished from the refugees, freely choose to live elsewhere and is capable of having a normal relationship with the authorities of his home country. The refugee is distinguished from a stateless person because he, unlike the stateless person, may still have a de jure national Status.

Sir John Hope Simpson has aptly defined-

> "The essential quality of a refugee is that he has sought refuge in a territory other than that in which fie was formerly resident as a result of political events which render his continued residence in his former territory .... impossible or intolerable".

As such, the main problem with refugee is they are a persistent embarrassment to the international legal community. The tension between the refugees and the conventional international order is the distinctive political dynamic of refugee status. It renders protection of the refugees a unique challenge for law and legal process, particularly once the refugee is in the State where he seeks refuge.

The present chapter deals with the brief historical outline of the evolution of the refugee definition. The purpose of following discussion is to examine who is a 'refugee' as defined by the various international instruments. How does he differ from a stateless person? What are the problems concerning the determination of the refugee status and how is this status be terminated? Finally, what is the procedure to determine the status of refugees -in case of large-scale influx ? The concern in this chapter is not with internal refugee who has moved from one part of the State to another, but with international political, and humanitarian refugees, who move from one State to another.

Refugee is not a concept of customary international law. Therefore, this law does not define him. He has been the subject of treaties and other international agreements. So, it is impossible to give one single definition which could be used ' in all circumstances. As Prof. Goedhart rightly observed that:

> "A sociological definition of the term 'refugee' differs from a legal one; the definition drafted for the purpose of the binding international agreement will look very different from the-definition adopted by an association with a humanitarian aim".

However, in general terms, a 'refugee' is usually thought of a person compelled to flee his state of origin or residence due to political troubles, persecution, famine or natural disaster.

## Refugees Defined in International Instruments: 1920-1950

Analysis of the international legal accords pertaining to refugees entered into between 1920 and 1950 reveals three distinct trends in refugee definition. From 1920 until 1935, refugees were defined in largely juridical terms. The juridical approach treats as refugees groups of persons outside their State of origin who have been effectively deprived of the formal protection of their government.

The social approach to refugee definition was dominant between 1935 and 1939. Refugees defined from the social perspective are the helpless casualties of broad-based social or political occurrences which separate them from this home society.

Refugees were defined in primarily individualistic terms between 1933 and 1950. A refugee by individualist standards is a person in search of an escape from perceived injustice of fundamental incompatibility with his home State.

So, the initial series of international refugee definitions were primarily concerned with the juridical phenomenon of refugeehood, that is, with the notion that the refugee is a member of a group that has no freedom of international movement because its members have been effectively deprived of the formal protection of their government.

Organised international action on behalf of refugees began in that year when the League of Nations was faced with the problem created by about the million refugees who had left Russia in consequence of Russian Revolution. The International Red Cross Committee appealed to the Council of the League of Nations in February 1921 to take action on behalf of the "Russian refugees scattered throughout Europe without legal protection or representation". The decision of the Red Cross to address the refugee crisis in juridical rather than strictly humanitarian terms prompted a positive response from the council. On June 27th 1921, the Council of the League of Nations decided to appoint a High Commissioner for Russian Refugees whose duty would be to co-ordinate the assistance given to those refugees by various countries.

Dr. Fridtjof Nansen was appointed High Commissioner on 20th August 1921. His tasks were-

- To define the legal status of refugees,
- To organise their repatriation or their allocation to the various countries, and
- To undertake relief work amongst them with the aid of philanthropic societies'.

The mandate of the High Commissioner was extended to Armenian refugees in 1924 and to Assyrian, Assyro-Chaldean and Turkish refugees in 1928. Between 1924 and 1929, the tasks of the High Commissioner in the field of relief of refugees were entrusted to the International Labour Office, while their protection remained his main responsibility. In 1929, both tasks were again combined in, the Office of the High Commissioner, which was placed under the authority of the Secretary General of the League of Nations.

However, the first international instrument to deal with the legal status of these refugees was signed in Geneva on June 30,1928. This agreement was worded in the form of resolutions recommending that the States accepting it, adopt certain measures for the protection of the Russian and Armenian refugees. This temporary arrangement-was supplanted by the regular convention relating to the International Status of Refugees signed at Geneva on October 28,1933. It also dealt with the other groups of refugees referred to above, but was only accepted by 8 states.

In 1936, when the Provisional Agreement concerning the Status of Refugees coming from Germany was adopted, the term 'refugee' covered all persons coming from Germany. However, a person did not qualify for Convention refugee status, if he had left Germany for reasons of purely personal conveniences'. During the conference in 1938, the term 'refugee' covers—

(a) Persons possessing or having possessed German nationality and not possessing any other nationality who are proved not to enjoy, in law or fact, the protection of the German Government.

(b) Stateless persons not covered by previous conventions or agreements who have left German territory after being established therein and who are proved not to enjoy, in law or in fact, the protection of the German Govt.

However, at the Bermuda Conference in 1943, it was decided that the protection should be extended to persons who :

> "As a result of events in Europe, have had to leave, or may have to leave, their countries of residence because of the danger to their lives or liberties on account of their race, religious or political beliefs."

The first formal reference to persecution as part of the refugee definition came in 1946 constitution of the International Refugee Organisation. The actual part of the constitution reads :

> "Persecution, or fear based on reasonable grounds of persecution because of race, religion, nationality or Political opinions, provided these opinions are not in conflict with the principles of the United Nations, as laid down in the Preamble of the Charter of the United Nations."

'Refugees', as defined by the constitution of the IRC, included victims of the Nazi, Fascist, or Quisling regimes which had opposed the United Nations, certain persons of

Jewish origin, or foreigners or stateless persons who had been victims of Nazi Persecution, as well as persons considered as refugees before the outbreak of the Second World War for reasons of race, religion, nationality or political opinion.

Prof. James C. Hathaway observes that the movement of refugee law away from principles of humanitarianism intensified between 1938 and 1950. In particular, the determination of refugee status on the basis of a broadly defined lack of protection came to an end. No longer was it enough to be a member of a group of displaced or stateless persons, rather, a particularized analysis of each claimants' motives for flight was requisite to recognition as a refugee.

The two major attempts by the United Nations to define a refugee were made in 1950 in drafting the Statute of the Office of the United Nations High Commissioner for Refugees" and in 1951, when the United Nations Conference of Plenipotentiaries adopted the Convention Relating to the Status of Refugees." In both cases a reasoned attempt was made to revise and consolidate previous instruments relating to the status of refugees. To this end both definitions begin by recognizing as refugees persons so A recognized by various Pre-war Arrangements and Conventions.

Art. I of the Statute provides that the United Nations High Commissioner for Refugees, acting under the authority of the General Assembly, shall assume the function of providing international protection under the auspices of the United Nations, to refugees, who, fall within the scope of the present Statute and of seeking permanent solutions for the problem of refugees by assisting Governments and- subject to the approval of the Governments concerned, private organizations to facilitate the voluntary repatriation of such refugees, or their assimilation within new national communities.

Art. 6-A of the Statute of the UNHCR lays down that the competence of the High Commissioner shall extend to-

(i) Any person who has been considered a refugee under the Arrangements of May 12, 1926 and of June 30, 1928 or under the Conventions of October 28, 1933 and February 10, 1938, the Protocol of September 14, 1939 or the constitution of the International Refugee Organisation.

(ii) Any person who, as a result of events occurring before January 1, 1951 and owing to well-founded fear of being persecuted for reasons of race, religion, nationality or political opinion, is outside the country of his nationality and is unable or, owing to such fear or for reasons other than personal convenience, is unwilling to avail himself of the protection of that country or who, not having a nationality and being outside the country of his former habitual residence, is unable or, owing to such fear or for reasons other than personal convenience, is unwilling to return to it.

Further 6-B of the said statute lays down as under:

> Any other person who is outside the country of his nationality, or if he has no nationality, the country of his former habitual residence, because he has or had well-founded fear of persecution by reason of his race, religion, nationality or political opinion and is unable or, because of such fear, is unwilling to avail himself of the protection of the governmental of the country of his nationality, or, if he has no nationality, to return to the country of his former habitual residence.

This description is of universal application, containing neither temporal nor geographical limitations. However, the UNHCR statute contains an apparent contradiction as observed by Prof. Guy S. Godwin-Gill" "on the one hand, it affirms that the work of the office shall relate, as a rule, to groups and categories of refugees. On the other hand, it proposes a definition of the refugee which is essentially individualistic, requiring case by case examination of subjective and objective elements".

In the 1951 Convention relating to the status of Refugees and for the purposes of that Convention, the applies under Article I-A, to any person who:

(1) Has been considered a refugee under the Arrangements of 12 May 1926 and 30 June 1928 or under the conventions of 28 October 1933 and 10 February 1938, the Protocol of 14 September 1939 or the Constitution of the International Refugee Organisation; and

(2) As a result of events occurring before 1 January 1951 and owing to well-founded fear of being persecuted for reasons of race, religion, nationality, membership of a particular social group or Political opinion, is outside the country of his nationality and is unable or, owing to such fear, is unwilling to avail himself of the protection of that country, or who not having a nationality and being outside the country of his former habitual residence as a result of such events, is unable or, owing to such fear, is unwilling to return to it".

The above Article I-A of the 1951 Convention covers two groups of persons who are considered as refugees for the purpose of its application:

The first group could be called "Statutory" refugees, i.e. persons who have already been considered as refugees under previous international agreements or under the Constitution of the IRO. The second group embraces persons who are accorded the status of a 'refugee' for the first time. It consists of two subgroups, one possessing a nationality and the other without a nationality. There are two conditions applicable to both groups:

(a) they must be outside the country of their nationality or of their habitual residence, and
(b) they must be there as a result of events which took place before January 1, 1951.

Persons with a nationality meeting these two tests are to be considered as refugees only if they are outside the country of their nationality owing to well-founded fear of being persecuted for reasons of race, religion, nationality, membership in a particular social group, or political opinion and are unable or owing to the fear of persecution, unwilling to avail themselves of the protection of the country of their nationality. Persons without nationality, meeting the first two tests, are considered refugees if they are unable or, owing to well-founded fear of persecution, unwilling to return to the country of their former habitual residence.

The Convention excludes from its application two groups those persons who receive protection or assistance from organs or agencies of the United Nations, other than the High Commissioner, during the time of the existence of such protection or assistance; those persons who, although they would normally come under the definition of a *refugee,* are not deemed worthy of international protection.

Realising the necessity of protecting the new refugees whose fear of persecution is not related to the events occurred before 1951, a Protocol relating to the status of Refugees was adopted and opened for signature in 1967 '21 which omitted temporal and geographical limitations on the definition of the term 'refugee' under the 1951 Refugee Convention. Article I of the 1967 Protocol defined a refugee as a person who:

> Owing to well-founded fear of being persecuted for reasons of race, religion, nationality, membership of a particular social group or political opinion, is outside the country of his nationality and its unable or, owing to such fear, is unwilling to avail himself of protection of that country; or who, not having a nationality and being outside the country of his former habitual residence, owing to such fear, is unwilling to return to it.

Thus, the Protocol had been set up to cope with the, problem of the limitation of the personal scope of the 1951 Convention, as it was felt "desirable that equal status should be enjoyed by all refugees covered by the definition in the convention irrespective of the definition of 1 January 1951". However, the definition contained within 1951 Convention clearly does not cover everyone outside his or her country, in a Situation of distress, and unable to return home. People may be unwilling or unable to return to their own country due to circumstances such as natural disasters-famines, floods or earthquakes which have rendered life there impossible. These circumstances, however, are not included within the criteria specified in the Convention definition. Hence, people in these situations are not refugees within the ambit of that definition.

Of course, it is to be noted that the 1951 Convention was primarily drawn upto deal with the situation of displaced persons in Europe immediately after the Second World War, and to provide protection for those persons. The States acceding to the Convention were anxious to make their obligations specific and to ensure that those obligations could not be extended indefinitely. Today, circumstances have changed and many people who need international protection of the kind provided by the convention do not fall within its ambit.

The essential purpose of the Convention is to provide for a legal regime which ensures protection to a group of persons who are in a particularly vulnerable situation. Article I of the Convention (combined with article I of the 1967 Protocol) defines a "refugee" as a person who-

> "owing to well founded fear of being persecuted for reasons of race, religion, nationality, membership of a particular social group or political opinion, is outside the country of this nationality and is unable, or owing to such fear, is unwilling to avail himself of the protection of that country, or who, not having a nationality and being outside the country of his former habitual residence as a result of such events, is unable or, owing to such fear, is unwilling to return to it".

Thus, a refugee is a person who is outside his or her country of origin (or habitual residence in case of statelessness) and who, owing to a well founded fear of persecution for reasons of race, religion, nationality, membership of a particular social group or political opinion, is unable or unwilling to avail himself or herself of the protection to which he or she is normally entitled from that country.

The decision as to whether a person is entitled to refugee status is taken by each State in accordance with its own established procedures, consistent with international standards, on the basis of the criteria laid down in Article 1 of the Convention. UNHCR plays a role in these procedures if and as requested, and is thus able to share its accumulated experience with Governments regarding status determination and the general handling of refugee problems. Such participation is in line with Article 35 for the Convention and the corresponding Article II of the Protocol.

**Cessation of Refugee Status**

Article 1C of the Convention provides that a person shall cease be a refugee

1. he or she has voluntarily re-availed himself or herself of the protection of the country of his or her nationality-,
2. having lost his or her nationality, he or she has voluntarily re-acquired it;
3. he or she has acquired a new nationality and enjoys the protection of the country of his or her new nationality;
4. he or she has voluntarily re-established himself or herself in the country which her or she left or outside which he or she remained owing to fear of persecution,
5. the circumstances in connection with which he or she has been recognised as a refugee have ceased to exist, and he or she can no longer continue to refuse the protection of the country of his or her nationality, or
6. he or she is without nationality, but because of a change of circumstances in connection with which he or she has been recognised as a refugee have ceased to exist, is able to return to his or her country of former habitual residence.

As such, a contracting State may resort to this provision to determine that the refugee status of an individual or a group has ceased. It should, however, be noted that there may nevertheless be circumstances in individual cases which could make it unreasonable to expect a person (or his or her family members) to return to the country of origin. Severely traumatised persons should not be forced to return to their country of origin.

**Exclusion from Refugee Status**

Article 1 of the Convention identifies, in Sections D, E and F, cases in which persons otherwise having the characteristics of refugees are excluded from refugee status. Such persons fall into three groups:

- the first group consists of persons already receiving protection or assistance from agencies or organs of the United Nations other than UNHCR. Such people include the Palestinians who, in parts of the Middle East, receive assistance from agencies or organs of the United Nations Relief and Works Agency for Palestine Refugees in the Near East (UNRWA),
- the second group consists of persons who are not considered to be in need of international protection. Those are persons who have been received in a country where they have been granted most of the rights normally enjoyed by nationals, short of formal citizenship. For example, people of German descent from Central Europe and the former Soviet Union, irrespective of nationality, are thus protected under the German Constitution, and are therefore not refugees under the 1951 Convention;
- the third group comprises categories of persons who are not considered to be deserving international protection, because there are serious reasons for considering that they have committed a crime against peace, a war crime or a crime against humanity, or a serious non-political crime outside the country of

> refuge prior to admission to that country as refugees; or they have been guilty of acts contrary to the purposes and principles of the United Nations.

In this book we have tried to make an assessment of refugee problem in human rights perspective. Its causes, magnitude, impact on world order and national and international approach to its mitigation are elaborately dealt with in the succeeding chapters of the book.

# 2

# Criteria for Claiming Refugee Status

> "Between the great things we cannot do and the small things we will not do ... the danger is that we shall do nothing."
>
> —*Henry G. Weaver*

## Alienage

The first element of Convention refugee status is that the claimant must be outside her country of origin. There is nothing intuitively obvious about this requirement: many if not most of the persons forced to flee their homes in search of safety remain within the boundaries of their state. Their plight may be every bit as serious as that of individuals who cross borders, yet the Convention definition of refugee status excludes internal refugees from the scope of global protection.

The strict insistence on this territorial criterion has prompted concern that there is a mismatch between the definition and the human suffering consequent to involuntary migration. In one sense, the exclusion of internal refugees is clearly unfair: it does not recognize the existence of social, legal, and economic barriers which make it impossible for all to escape to international protection. The Convention definition of refugee status therefore responds in a less than even-handed way to the protection needs of persons similarly at risk of persecution.

There is a threefold historical rationale for the requirement that only persons outside their state be eligible for Convention refugee status. First, the Convention was drafted with a specific purpose in the context of limited international resources. Its intent was not to relieve the suffering of all involuntary migrants, but rather to deal *"only with the problem of legal protection and status."* Its goal was to assist a subset of involuntary migrants composed of persons who were "outside their own countries (and) who lacked the protection of a government", and who consequently required short-term surrogate international rights until they acquired new or renewed national protection. Internal refugee displacements, while of humanitarian note, "were separate problems of a different character", the alleviation of which would demand a more sustained commitment of resources than was available to the international community.

Second, there was a very practical concern that the inclusion of internal refugees in the international protection regime might prompt states to attempt to shift responsibility for the well-being of large parts of their own population to the world community. The obligations of states under the Convention would thereby be increased, as a result of which fewer states would be likely to participate in the Convention regime.

Third and most fundamental, there was anxiety that any attempt to respond to the needs of internal refugees would constitute an infringement of the national sovereignty of the state within which the refugee resided. Refugee law, as a part of international human rights law, constitutes a recent and carefully constrained exception to the long-standing rule of exclusive jurisdiction of states over their inhabitants. While it was increasingly accepted in the early 1950s that the world community had a legitimate right to set standards and scrutinize the human rights record of the various countries, it was unthinkable that refugee law would intervene in the territory of a state to protect citizens from their own government. The best that could be achieved within the context of the accepted rules of international law was the sheltering of such persons as were able to liberate themselves from the territorial jurisdiction of a persecutory state.

None of the three factors which dictated the exclusion of internal refugees -limited resources, concern about state participation, or respect for sovereignty-was so much a matter of conceptual principle, as it was a reflection of the limited reach of international law. As Andrew Shacknove has observed, *"alienage is an unnecessary condition for establishing refugee status. It ... is a subset of a broader category: the physical access of the international community to the unprotected person."* In other words, the physical presence of the unprotected person outside her country of origin is not a constitutive element of her refugeehood, but is rather a practical condition precedent to placing her within the effective scope of international protection.

The territorial dimension of the Convention definition of refugee status, then, was dictated by the extant authority of international law. Its purpose was not to divide involuntary migrants into those who are worthy of assistance and those who are not deserving, but was instead to define the scope of refugee law in a realistic, workable way. As the authority of the international community over human rights has increased with the passage of time, so too has the reach of refugee law expanded, at least tentatively, to protect some internal refugees.

First, since 1972 the United Nations High Commissioner for Refugees has been called on to provide material assistance to various groups of refugees within their national boundaries. This assistance has been premised on the concurrence of the state concerned and the willingness of the international community to provide funding, but is nonetheless indicative of an enhanced recognition of an international role in the protection of internal refugees Second, and more dramatic, is the establishment of orderly-departure programs in collaboration with refugee-producing states, whereby refugees may make application from within their country of origin resettlement abroad under international auspices.

Both of these developments bear witness to Shacknove's position that the territorial limitation in the Convention refugee definition is a function of "the art of the possible", which may decrease in importance as unprotected persons still within their states become more accessible to the international community. The alienage requirement raises a number of specific issues.

First, must an individual leave her country as a result of fear of persecution, or may she successfully claim Convention refugee status if her fear arises at a time when she is already abroad? Second, does it matter if the putative refugee left her country with or without the official authorization of her state? Third, must a refugee claim status in the country nearest her home, or in the first state to which she flees? Fourth, what is the implication of entry into an asylum state by fraudulent means or in contravention of applicable immigration laws? Finally, what country must an individual be outside of in order to qualify for Convention refugee status where she is, for example, possessed of dual or multiple nationality, or conversely is stateless?

## Refugees Sur Place

The Convention refugee definition does not distinguish between persons who flee their country in order to avoid the prospect of persecution and those who, while already abroad, determine that they cannot or will not return by reason of the risk of persecution in their state of nationality or origin. By virtue of its requirement that the claimant *"is outside the country of his nationality . . . "* the Convention protects refugees *sur place* on an equal footing with those who cross a border after the risk of persecution is already apparent. This position is consonant with the general rule that the territorial requirement of the Convention definition is intended to identify those involuntary migrants within the effective reach of international law: whether already present or arriving in a foreign state, the refugee claimant is clearly able to benefit from protection against return.

## Claims Grounded in Events in the Country of Origin

The classic *sur place* refugee claim derives from a significant change of circumstances in the country of origin at a time when the claimant is abroad for reasons wholly unrelated to a need for protection. At the time of departure from her state, she may have intended only to vacation, study, or do business abroad, and then to return home. If, however, events subsequent to her departure would put her at risk of serious harm upon return home, she may claim protection as a Convention refugee.

For example, the decision in *Chaudri v. Minister of Employment and Immigration* involved a Pakistani citizen who had been an activist in the ruling People's Party of Pakistan prior to the military overthrow of 1979. Mr. Chaudri had been in Canada for some three years prior to the coup. In 1980, he learned that the new military government of Pakistan had issued a politically inspired warrant for his arrest that could lead to indefinite detention. The Federal Court of Appeal held that he was, properly considered a Convention refugee sur place since his fear of persecution, while not extant at the time of his departure from Pakistan, was nonetheless well-founded in subsequent events.

The same result was reached in the case of *Almaz Isebella Kebede Fernandes,* involving an Ethiopian student abroad when the military ousted Emperor Haile Selassi. Her father, the Emperor's bodyguard, had been killed by the military, and all of her immediate family was either in detention or in receipt of asylum in other countries. In the circumstances, the Immigration Appeal Board found her to be a Convention refugee in that she "could not possibly return to her country at the present time and expect to be treated favourably by the military junta." A variant of the classical *sur place* situation involves the dramatic intensification of pre-existing factors since departure from one's home country.

While distinguishable from the first category by the fact that the claimant may have been aware of, or even motivated to depart by, disturbing events in her home country, these cases are characterized by an escalation of events post-departure which is sufficient to give rise to a reasonable risk of persecution upon return. In a series of decisions involving Eritrean seamen, the Immigration Appeal Board found that the long-standing mistreatment of this ethnic group by Ethiopian authorities had so intensified during the claimants' time abroad that it was reasonable for them to conclude that their lives or liberty would be at risk upon return to their country. Similarly, in the case *of Thillainathan Srikanthan* the Board determined that *"recent events in the State of Sri Lanka lead the Board to believe that the applicant, although marginally involved in political events at the time of his residence in that country, may encounter some problems if he were to be returned . . . at the present time the applicant has good reason to fear persecution"* [Emphasis added]. The Immigration Appeal Board also considered the intensification of harm doctrine in a number of cases involving allegations of increased governmental hostility toward Sikhs in the State of Punjab, but found that the changes in government policy there did not yet amount to a sufficiently serious risk of harm.

**Claims Grounded in the Asylum Seeker's Activities Abroad**

In addition to claims grounded in either new circumstances or a dramatic intensification of pre-existing conditions in the country of origin, a *sur place* claim to refugee status may also be based on the activities of the refugee claimant since leaving her country. International law recognizes that if while abroad an individual expresses views or engages in activities' which jeopardize the possibility of safe return to her state, she may be considered a Convention refugee.

The key issues are whether the activities abroad are likely to have come to the attention of the authorities in the claimant's country of origin and, if so, how they are likely to be viewed and responded to. The leading Canadian authority on this point is the decision of the Federal Court of Appeal in *Mohamed Ahmed Urur v. Minister of Employment and Immigration.* Responding to the Immigration Appeal Board's refusal to receive photographic evidence of the claimant's participation in a demonstration in Ottawa in front of the embassy of his country of origin, the Court held that "[t]his refusal by the Board was manifestly wrong. An alien in Canada may be a refugee as a consequence of facts which have occurred since his arrival," A *sur place* claim to refugee status was recognized, for example, in the case of *Irfam Ismailovski,* who had helped to publish antigovernment propaganda directed to the

Albanian exile community in Canada, thereby placing himself at risk of incarceration by his home authorities.

Other very similar claims have, however; been rejected. The Board in *Carlos Armando Guerra Morales* denied refugee status to a Chilean emigre journalist who had been *"since his arrival, engaged in many activities directed against the "present regime in his native country."* Involvement with politically hostile emigrant groups has likewise been looked upon with scepticism, even where such activity has been clearly publicized. The Immigration Appeal Board has asserted that *"it is not reasonable that a person may place himself in jeopardy with the laws of his country ... and thereby claim special status if it is that act itself which creates the claim for refugee status."*

Canadian decision-makers are not alone in taking this position. Except where, foreign policy goals are served, American authorities have also rejected most claims grounded in political activity in the United States. Because persons might engage in oppositional activity strictly or primarily with the intention of placing themselves at risk, there is concern that such claims present a clear opportunity for abuse by persons who are not really in need of protection. Such an absolutist preoccupation with the possibility of fraud ignores the basic right of all persons to be free to express themselves, to associate with whomever they wish, to pursue the development of their own personalities.

Logically, visitors from abroad who exercise their right to speak out against - their home government, who associate with opposition emigrant groups, or who otherwise engage in lawful activity perceived by their state of origin to be inappropriate should be protected from return where there is a serious risk of persecution as a result of those actions. Since the voluntary issuance of the challenge to the home state is clearly lawful in and of itself, any reticence to acknowledge the validity of a claim to protection in such circumstances "chills an alien's constitutionally protected freedom of expression."

Because the expression of oppositional opinion is lawful, there is no good reason to focus on the question of voluntariness *per se.* The conceptual awkwardness in recognizing these claims derives rather from the fact that not all instances of voluntary alienation give rise to a risk of harm which can readily be linked to one of the five forms of civil or political status set out in the Convention. Specifically, it is legitimate to grant refugee status in this type of case only in sofar as the claimant's post-departure activities may genuinely be seen to reflect her true political opinion, or alternatively where there is evidence that those activities may lead to the attribution to her of a political opinion by authorities in her home state. Otherwise whatever consequences ensue from her actions abroad are the result only of her unfounded or untruthful assertions, a predicament outside the scope of the Convention definition.

In the case of persons who have chosen to be politically active in their state of origin, the authenticity of the political opinion underlying the Activism is generally assumed. This is sensible, because an individual would be unlikely to make insincere attacks on her state at a time when she remains within its grasp. The ability of the state to exert control and to punish is an implied barometer of authenticity. In contrast, an individual *outside* the jurisdiction of her state of origin may be subject to no such automatic and effective control mechanism. It is thus more readily conceivable that an oppositional stance could be assumed simply for the purpose of fabricating a claim to refugee status," and thus not reflect a political opinion as required by the definition. The challenge, then, is to respond to this real evidentiary difference without being dismissive of such protection needs as may arise from the expression of sincerely held convictions at a time when an individual is abroad.

This can be done by canvassing a number of issues. First, does the claimant retain close personal connections to family, friends, or institutions in her home state? In sofar as such a nexus exists, it affords a surrogate indicator of sincerity, as the claimant would be less likely to engage in unfounded opposition where persons who are important to her are at risk. Second, are the claimant's statements or actions abroad consistent with her behaviour prior to departure? If so, the consistency affords some evidence of veracity. If there is no consistency, are there valid reasons to explain the claimant's openness or change of views once abroad? Third, can the firmness of the claimant's newly expressed convictions be tested? To the extent that she has a clear understanding of relevant concerns and issues and has become significantly involved in their propagation, it is more likely that she genuinely embraces the belief underlying her statements or actions.

It does not follow, however, that all persons whose activities abroad are not genuinely demonstrative of oppositional Political opinion are outside the refugee definition. Even when it is evident that the voluntary statement or action was fraudulent in that it was prompted primarily by an intention to secure asylum, the consequential imputation to the claimant of a negative political opinion by authorities in her home state may nonetheless bring her within the scope of the Convention definition. Since refugee law is fundamentally concerned with the provision of protection against unconscionable state action, an assessment should be made of any potential harm to be faced upon return because of the fact of the non-genuine political activity engaged in while abroad.

This issue is most poignantly raised when it is alleged that the fact of having made an unfounded asylum claim *may per se* give rise to a serious risk of persecution. While these cases provide perhaps the most obvious , potential for "bootstrapping", there must nonetheless be a clear acknowledgment and assessment of any risk to basic human rights upon return which may follow from the state's imputation of an unacceptable political opinion to the claimant. The mere fact that the claimant might suffer some form of penalty may not be sufficiently serious to constitute persecution, but there are clearly situations where the consequence of return may be said to give rise to a well-founded fear of persecution.

For example, in Slawomir Krzystof Hubicki evidence was adduced that under then-prevailing Polish criminal law, the claimant would face imprisonment of up to eight years because he had made a refugee claim in Canada. In such situations, the basis of claim is not the fraudulent activity or assertion itself, but is rather the political opinion of disloyalty imputed to the claimant by her state. Where such an imputation exists, the gravity of consequential harm and other definitional criteria should be assessed to determine whether refugee status is warranted.

*Departure from the State of Origin*

The second aspect of alienage is concerned with the means by which the refugee claimant exited her country of origin. First, can the fact of illegal departure or may abroad be said to give rise per se to a genuine risk of serious harm? Second, to what extent are issues of authorized or unauthorized departure probative of the genuineness of the claim to refugee status? Third, can a refugee claim arise where the state of origin not only authorizes, but in some sense facilitates the claimant's departure?

### *Illegal Departure or Stay Abroad*

The mere fact that an individual either departs her country or stays abroad without authorization does not always entitle her to refugee status. However, if two conditions are met, a genuine refugee claim may be established.

First, the country of origin must punish unauthorized exit or stay abroad in a harsh or oppressive manner. The prospect of, reasonable penalties for breach of a fairly administered passport law, for example, is not a harm of sufficient gravity to warrant protection as a refugee. On the other hand, where the sanctions for illicit travel abroad are so severe that they effectively negate the fundamental human right to leave and return to one's country, there *is* the basis for a claim to refugee status.

Second, the illegal departure or stay abroad must either be explicitly politically motivated, or the state of origin must view the unauthorized departure or stay abroad as an implied political statement of disloyalty or defiance. Whether by law or administrative practice, it must be clear that the home country disapproves of illicit emigration, and views those who breach its rules on exit or travel abroad as non-conforming dissidents. This perspective is exemplified by those societies in which it is considered a crime to seek to withdraw from the national community by emigration, and which brand all those who leave as traitors. Claims should not be denied simply because they are prompted by an intention to secure asylum abroad. As in the case of *sur place* claims based on post-departure voluntary acts, refugee status should be recognized where there is a prospect of serious harm upon return as the result of the imputation to the claimant of an unacceptable political opinion.

In so far as a refugee claimant can meet this two-part test, she falls within the scope of the Convention definition. She reasonably fears persecution because of her home government's established practice of harshly oppressive punishment. The reason she is at risk is moreover directly related to the political opinion that her government attributes to her unauthorized departure or stay, or to its view that her disloyal behavior has set her fundamentally apart from the national community.

Recent practice in North America has been less generous to persons who leave or remain outside their country illegally. In the United States, the individual's motives at the time of flight are viewed as determinative, what ever the position taken by the state of origin. Thus, unless the refugee leaves her country for specifically political reasons, she is not a refugee. Canadian courts have accepted a similar fear of reprisals for unauthorized departure or stay may be invoked as an auxiliary ground of claim, but is not sufficient to meet the refugee definition in and of itself.

The Immigration Appeal Board consistently noted that -violating the laws of one's country and having to face the consequences does not make one a refugee. Even where the penalties for the breach of controls on emigration are clearly inordinate, the Board refused to bend. For example, not withstanding evidence that Polish law would impose a five-year prison term for illegal exit, it was held that " *... if [the claimant] were to be imprisoned for leaving his country without proper authorization this, would not be considered persecution - but rather prosecution.*" Similarly, even though it was shown that illegal departees from the Soviet Union "*. . . under Russian* *law have committed treason and are subject to heavy penalties: on their return", it was decided that " [s]erious as this is for them, it is not persecution as defined in the Convention but the consequence of breaking Russian law."* This refusal to examine the substance of the state's response to unauthorized exit or sojourn (rather than just its form) is not in keeping with the Convention. Extreme, clearly unreasonable penalties/or the breach of travel restrictions convert what might otherwise have, been routine prosecution into the type of serious harm encompassed by the notion of persecution.

The often callous disregard for the plight of persons who face severe penalties for illegal departure or stay abroad is further evinced by the Immigration Appeal Board's view that because the potential sanctions are the same for all nationals of the country of origin, they are inherently non-persecutory. It is simply incorrect to argue that the pervasive nature of the restriction makes refugee protection unviable or inappropriate. By way of comparison, many societies have rules of universal application against freedom of expression. Refugee law does not purport to assist all persons who live within these societies, but rather only those whose defiance of the generalized rule has placed them at risk of serious harm. Similarly, only the minority of persons at risk in consequence of broadly based migration restrictions - namely, those who have contravened the standards - merits protection as refugees. It is not, however, sensible to ignore the reality of the minority genuinely at peril simply because any member of the home society could, if similarly situated, also become at risk.

**Inferences Based on the Legality of Departure**

A related question is the extent to which issues of authorized or unauthorized departure are probative of the genuineness *of* a claim to refugee status. The general rule, of course, is that if a person faces the risk of serious harm, the means by which she left her country of origin is essentially irrelevant An individual may depart her country without impediment, even travel on a valid passport, and still be a genuine refugee if the balance of the evidence in favour of recognition as a refugee is compelling. Moreover, the Federal Court of Appeal has held unequivocally that illegal departure, even involving forged documentation, is also no bar to a refugee claim. In *Benjamin Attakora v. Minister of Employment and Immigration,* the Court noted:

> ... [T]he Board found that the applicant's credibility was weakened by his statement that, while on the plane to Canada, he destroyed a passport, Canadian visitor's visa and airline ticket, all of which were in the name of a friend and had been used by him in order to get away. The Board, after noting that the applicant had said that he destroyed the documents because he was afraid that, if they were discovered, he might be arrested and sent back, concluded, without more, that this element of his testimony lacked credibility.

The Board's finding on this Point is, to say the least, Puzzling. There is certainly nothing inherently incredible in a refugees saying that he destroyed false documents in order to avoid detection and arrest once they had served their purpose. In the circumstances of this case, the destruction of such documents could not have had any conceivable relevance to any issue which the Board has to decide. I can only conclude that the Board's insistence upon its significance is founded upon some erroneous view of the law. Does the Board think that only persons who arrive with their travel documents in order can be refugees? Or that those who arrive with false documents have some obligation to preserve them?

Nonetheless, there are two situations where it is appropriate to consider information on the mode of departure.

First, evidence of difficulty in securing official permission to leave may be probative of a negative relationship between the claimant and her state, and thus corroborate other evidence tending to show-a genuine risk of harm in *Joseph Khouri,* for example, the Board looked to Syria's refusal of an exit visa to the claimant in order to substantiate the assertion that certain actions, which might otherwise have been politically ambiguous, were viewed by the government to have been traitorous. Too, evidence that bribery or influence was required in order to secure travel documents may infer the absence of a normal relationship between the claimant and her state, and thereby support a claim to refugee status. In *Shahram Nassirbake,* for example, the Board acknowledged the probative value of the Iranian claimant's need to pay a substantial sum to be smuggled out of his country, in view of the government's policy of refusing passports to its opponents.

Second and conversely, where the evidence of serious risk is less than clear-cut, evidence of undue ease of departure tends to discredit a claim to fear serious harm at the hands of the state. At least in countries that have sophisticated bureaucracies and information storage and retrieval systems, issuance of a passport or exit visa may indicate that the government has no particular concern to persecute the claimant. In the case of *Oscar Manuel Diaz Duran,* for example, the Immigration Appeal Board legitimately questioned the credibility of the Chilean claimant's vague assertion of risk on the ground that he had been issued a valid passport and exit visa, in contrast to his government's established practice of refusing travel documents to its political opponents. In *Bakhshish Gill Singh,* the Board observed that it had

> *. . . heard many accounts of Indian police incompetence in refugee determination cases, but there is a limit to such claimed incompetence beyond which credibility disappears. In this connection, it is hard to believe that Mr. Gill would have succeeded in obtaining a "no objection certificate" and an extension of his passport, quite apart from succeeding in getting through controls at Delhi airport, were there any serious desire on the part of the authorities to arrest him.*

Evidence of this kind, whether positive or negative, is not however determinative, but should rather be weighed together with other facts to discern the true extent of the risk faced by the refugee claimant. There is an unfortunate tendency to be reflexively dismissive of claimants who have freely exited their country or who possess valid travel documents. Suspicion is particularly high in the case of persons who have been actively assisted to leave their country. Yet in even these situations where the refugee's departure is facilitated by the state of origin, a genuine claim to refugee status can be established.

As Foighel has noted, Convention refugee status is fundamentally a function of the risk faced by the claimant, not of her mode of departure; state practice has not resulted in the generalized denial of protection to refugees who were assisted to leave by their home state; geographical or political limitations may mean that for some refugees the collaboration of their government is the only means of escape; and the extensive exclusion clauses of the Convention make no reference to the issue of the facilitation of departure by home authorities. In the result, the role of evidence on mode of departure should be carefully confined to situations of evidentiary ambiguity, and should not be allowed to override the fundamental concern to identify persons who would be at genuine risk of serious harm upon return to their state of origin.

**Persons with Dual or Multiple Nationality**

It is an underlying assumption of refugee law that wherever available, national protection takes precedence over international protection. In the drafting of the Convention, delegates were clear in their view that no person should be recognized as a refugee unless she is either unwilling or unable to avail herself of the protection of *all* countries of which she is a national. Even if an individual has a genuine fear of persecution in one state of nationality, she may not benefit from refugee status if she is a citizen of .another country that is prepared to afford her protection.

This principle of the Convention, is not explicitly incorporated in the *Immigration Act*. However, the courts have seen fit to exclude, for example, the claim of an at risk citizen and resident of Angola who retained Portuguese citizenship by virtue of his birth in that country. The fear of return of a Turkish national was also examined from the perspective of the risk he would face in Australia, a country whose citizenship he had acquired through naturalization during childhood. Even where the dual citizen has never set foot in her second country of nationality, refugee law requires an assessment of the degree of risk, if any, in that state as a prerequisite to international protection. This principle was recently affirmed by the Federal Court of Appeal in *Attorney General of Canada v. Patrick Francis Ward*. Explicitly citing the second paragraph of Article I (A)(2) of the Convention, which, while "not binding upon us since it has not been incorporated into Canadian law, is persuasive as forming a logical construction of the Convention refugee definition" the Court held:

> ... [I]f it is found that he has more than one country of nationality the claimant is obliged to establish his unwillingness to avail himself of the protection of each

of his countries of nationality before he can be considered to be a Convention refugee.

The major caveat to the principle of deferring to protection by a state of citizenship is the need to ensure *effective,* rather than merely formal, nationality. It is not enough, for example, that the claimant carries a second passport from a non-persecutory state if that state is not in fact willing to afford protection against return to the country of persecution. While it is appropriate to presume a willingness on the part of a country of nationality to protect in the absence of evidence to the contrary, facts that call into question the existence of basic protection against return must be carefully assessed.

In the case of *Harbans Rai Singh,* for example, the Immigration Appeal Board dismissed the applicant's alleged fear of persecution in his country of birth, India, on the ground that he possessed a British passport, and could accordingly expect to be protected by the United Kingdom. Evidence was adduced that the claimant's passport had been altered to delete his right of abode in the United Kingdom, thus raising the obvious possibility that the claimant's British nationality would provide him with less than fully effective protection. In these circumstances, the Board should have satisfied itself that its reliance on apparent second nationality was warranted before dismissing the claim.

In *James Patrick Gillen* the Board treated the claimant's apparent right to qualify for a British passport as sufficient to constitute both his country of citizenship, the Republic of Ireland, and the United Kingdom as countries of reference. There was no evidence that the claimant had ever been admitted to British territory outside Northern Ireland; moreover, the claimant gave uncontradicted testimony that entry to the United Kingdom had in fact been refused to other persons similarly situated. . The dilemma here is a logical extension of the concern to ensure effective nationality before assessing the adequacy of a *refugee claim:* only the degree of risk in those states that are known to be obliged to allow the re-entry of the claimant is relevant, as it is to one of those states that the putative refugee would- in most cases be sent back if not admitted to the country of refuge.

**Stateless Persons**

Refugee law exists to interpose the protection of the international system where a domestic government fails to protect an individual or collectivity under its national jurisdiction. The position of stateless persons is thus anomalous: Are all stateless persons refugees because by definition they do not benefit from national protection? Or conversely are stateless persons excluded from refugee status because their dilemma stems not from the failure of a national government to protect them, but rather from the absence state that can be said to have a duty of protection toward them?

This conceptual confusion is historically explicable. In the first phase of international refugee law, formal statelessness was a condition precedent to recognition as a refugee. The expanded focus of refugee law in the years leading up to the Second World War recognized *de facto* lack of protection as an equally compelling basis for international protection, but continued to protect stateless persons adrift in the international system as refugees. The divorce *of de jure* statelessness and refugee status came only during the drafting of the 1951 Convention.

The background study prepared by the Secretary General in 1949 proposed a revised and consolidated convention relating to the status of all persons without national protection. The Economic and Social Council approved the drafting of a convention which would-extend comprehensive humanitarian protection to both persons who lacked formal or *de jure* protection ("stateless persons") and persons who lacked *de facto* Protection, notwithstanding their retention of a particular nationality ("refugees"). The Conference of Plenipotentiaries, however, was of the view that refugees presented a more serious problem of humanitarian need: the problems of stateless persons were characterized as distinct, less urgent than the needs of refugees, and fundamentally giving rise to less of a social problem than the international protection of refugees. As such, it was agreed to restrict the scope of the Convention to those persons who required protection from a state to which they were formally returnable, and to leave the problems of the stateless population to be dealt with by a later and less comprehensive conventional regime.

It is thus clear that statelessness per se does not give rise to a claim to refugee status. On the other hand, the drafters of the Convention were equally unequivocal in their view that stateless persons could, in some situations, qualify as refugees. Where a stateless person has been admitted to a given country with a view to continuing residence of some duration, and subsequently finds herself in a position of being deprived of the protection of that state, she may find herself in a predicament comparable to that of a refugee with a nationality. This is only so, however, when the stateless person can be said to have a country of "former habitual residence" in the sense of a state that has evinced some degree of willingness to allow her to remain in its territory and to which she would be returnable if refugee protection were not granted.

To qualify as a refugee, then, the stateless person must

stand in a relationship to a state which is broadly comparable to the relationship between a citizen and her country of nationality. Because tile notion of a "former habitual residence" is intended to establish a point of reference for stateless refugee claimants that is the functional equivalent of a country of nationality, it implies some degree of formal responsibility for protection of the putative refugee.

A purposive interpretation of "former habitual residence" focuses on the nature of the ties between the claimant and countries in which she has resided, with a particular view to the identification of one or more Countries to which she is readmissible. Since refugee law is essentially a means of preventing the sending back of an individual to a state in which a risk of persecution exists, the proper point of reference is the country to which the claimant would normally be expected to return if not admitted to the asylum state. Under this rubric, Atle Grahl-Madsen's argument that country of former habitual residence should usually be equated with the state in which the stateless claimant first experienced persecution is not fully sustainable.

The country from which flight first occurred in often the state to which the refugee claimant retains the greatest formal legal ties, simply because subsequent states of residence which admitted her on the basis of her fear of persecution may not have granted her an unconditional right to return. On the other hand, the refugee claimant may have as strong or stronger formal ties to some other country or countries, in which case the claim to need protection should be assessed in relation to any and all countries to which she is formally returnable. This position respects the need for symmetrical treatment of persons with and without nationality, since in the case of the former group the Convention requires proof of lack of protection in all states of nationality.

Conversely, where the stateless refugee claimant has no right to return to her country of first persecution or to any other state, she cannot qualify as a refugee because she is not at risk of return to persecution, Assessment of the claimant's fear of returning to the country of first persecution is a nonsensical exercise, as she could not be sent back there In any event. Thus, when it is determined that the claimant does not have a right to return to any state, and does not therefore have a country of "former habitual residence", her needs should be addressed within the context, of the conventional regime for stateless persons rather than under refugee law.

Canadian practice has not clearly interpreted "former habitual residence" in the context of applications by stateless persons, but has defined the notion in relation to prior protection. First, the case law has required a significant period of defacto residence in the putative state of reference: one year appears to be accepted as a reasonable threshold standard, although most relevant decisions have in fact involved persons who resided in a foreign state for several years. Second, former habitual residence implies defacto abode, and not Merely ongoing transient presence Third, and most important, a state is a country of former habitual residence only if the claimant is legally able to return there. These indicia conform to the basic tenets of the concept of former habitual residence in international law, and provide the basis for a jurisprudence interpreting the criteria for determining when a stateless person may properly invoke the protection of refugee law.

**Persecution**

The refugee claimant must apprehend a form of harm which can be characterized as "persecution". This chapter examines the basis for the choice of persecution as the key definitional criterion in the Convention, and attempts to sketch a framework for determining when particular forms of mistreatment are of sufficient gravity to be classified as persecutory. This chapter is concerned with the substantive nature of the harm that refugee law is intended to confront.

The persecution standard evolved from the legitimate concern first stated in the 1938 Convention concerning the Status of Refugees coming from Germany' to exclude from protection those persons who were leaving their country for "reasons of purely personal convenience." The Constitution of the International Refugee Organization rephrased this principle in positive terms, and required the putative refugee to show "valid objections" to returning to her country of origin, which might include fear of persecution. The modern Convention, in turn, adopted the basic approach of the IRO precedent, but made persecution the exclusive benchmark for international' refugee status.

While it is true that the persecution-based standard permitted the identification of the victims of Nazism, it also spoke to the ideology-charged atmosphere which dominated the thinking of the Western states that prepared the Convention. The malleable persecution-based standard could be interpreted to embrace most of the emigrant dissidents from adversary states in the East Bloc, and would thus promote the immigration of Eastern Europeans to Western states then experiencing acute manpower shortages. Moreover, because a finding that a refugee claimant faces the possibility of persecution implies censure of the state of origin, each recognition of refugee status would simultaneously support efforts to stigmatize as injurious the political systems in the Communist' countries of origin.

Our continuing reliance on the persecution-based standard in an age when refugee states of origin and destination are frequently politically compatible has compromised the ability of refugee law to afford broadly based protection. In contrast to the cold war assumption of valid reasons for departure, refugee recognition today may be denied for reasons of foreign policy, or at least be conditioned by an unspoken view that an allied state is unlikely to act in a persecutory way. As Goran Melander has noted, "[R]ather than expose itself to the disapproval of the country of origin, a government may deny a person the status of refugee." The challenge is to recast the notion of "persecution" in a manner which is consonant with modern political realities, and which genuinely enables governments to conceive of refugee protection as a humanitarian act which ought not to be a cause of tension between states.

# 3

# Regional Instruments

> "The only people who achieve much are those who want knowledge so badly that they seek it while the condi-tions are still unfavorable. Favorable conditions never come."
>
> —*Clive Staples Lewis*

It is in Africa where the international community is confronted with the most complex challenge and to which it has to devote a major share of its social and economic, resources. The flow of refugees in Africa became an acute problem in the 1960s, coinciding with the struggle for an attainment of independence by most African States. Since the establishment of the Organisation of African Unity (OAU) in 1963, the refugee question has been of concern to the Organisation. It was decided to draw up a convention which should reflect and resolve the specific concerns of the African refugee problem.

Here it may be mentioned that the 1951 Convention and the 1967 Protocol remain the principal international instruments benefitting refugees, and the definition which they offer has been expressly adopted in a variety of regional arrangements aimed at further improving the situation of recognised refugees.

In October 1967, a Conference on Legal, Economic and Social aspects of African Refugee Problems was held in Addis Ababa. However, the recommendations on the matter, adopted by the Conference, only stated that:

> "In addition to the definition contained in the 1951 United Nations Convention relating to the Status of Refugees, As extended by the United Nations Protocol of 1967, African States should take into account the specific aspects of African refugee situations with regard in particular to the definition 'of an African Refugee."

In June 1968, the OAU Refugee Commission met in Addis Ababa in order to complete a final draft of an African Refugee Convention which was finally adopted by the Assembly of Heads of State and Government in September 1969. This is the first internationally accepted agreement which issues absolute and unqualified requirements stipulating that no refugee shall be subjected to measures, such as rejection at the frontier, which might compel him to return or remain in a territory where life, physical integrity or liberty would be threatened.

The most interesting aspect of the OAU Convention is its two-fold definition of a 'refugee'. It incorporates the same definition as in the 1951 Convention without the dateline and without the possibility of geographical limitation. At the same time it includes explicitly persons who are victims of man-made disasters like international armed conflicts or civil wars etc.

As per the provision of this Convention-the term 'refugee' shall also apply to every person who, owing to external aggression, Occupation, foreign domination or events seriously disturbing public order in either part or the whole of his country of origin or nationality, is compelled to leave his place of habitual residence in order to seek refuge in another place outside his country of origin or nationality.

So, unlike the two universal conventions, this one does not speak of subjective fear of the individual, but refers only to the objective conditions prevailing in the country of the refugee.

**The 1966 Bangkok Principles**

In the definition of the term 'refugee' given in Article I of the 1966 Principles concerning Treatment of Refugees adopted by the Asian-African Legal Consultative Committee, the term 'refugee' is applied to:

> "A person who, owing to persecution or well-founded fear of persecution for reasons of race, colour, religion, Political belief or membership of a Political Social group-
>
> (a) leaves the state of which he is a national, or the country of his nationality, the state or country of which he is a habitual resident; or
>
> (b) being outside such state or country is unable or unwilling to return to it or to avail himself of its protection."

Two explanations attached to this Article state that:

(1) the dependents of a refugee shall be deemed to be refugees; and

(2) the expression leaves' includes voluntary as -well as involuntary leaving.

**Europe**

The Council of Europe adopted several instruments concerning refugees. Some of the most important are:

(a) European Agreement on the Abolition of Visas for Refugees (1959);

(b) Resolution 14 (1967) on Asylum to Persons in Danger of persecution;

(c) European Agreement on Transfer of Responsibility for Refugees (1980);

(d) Recommendation on the Harmonization of National Procedures Relating to Asylum (1981);

(e) Recommendation on the protection of persons satisfying the criteria in the Geneva Convention who are riot formally Refugees (1984); and

(f) Dublin Convention (1900).

**Latin America**

Latin American States have a long tradition of providing humanitarian treatment to persons seeking protection and asylum. A century ago, the 'Treaty of International Penal Law' was signed in Montevideo on 23rd January 1889 on the occasion of the first South American Congress on Private International Law.

It contains the first provision on asylum in international treaty law, with a stipulation (Art. 16) to the effect that 'asylum for persons persecuted for Political crimes is inviolable'.

The next important instrument on asylum was signed in 1954 at Caracas which is known as the Caracas Convention on Territorial Asylum,

However, in the 1980s, the outbreak of Civil strife in Central America resulted in massive exoduses of million persons to neighbouring countries in search of protection and assistance.

Responding to the demands created by this unprecedented

situation, the countries concerned initiated a process of identification and implementation of humanitarian measures for the protection and assistance of the refugees. The process was advanced further with the holding of a colloquium[27] in Cartagena, Columbia in November 1984 where the Cartagena Declaration on Refugees, which contains a set of Principles and criteria for the protection of and assistance to refugee, was adopted.

Recognizing the particular characteristics of the flow of displaced persons in the region, the Cartagena Declaration extends the notion of refugees to include, apart from those covered by the universal refugees concept, also other externally displaced persons who are in need of protection and assistance. Consequently, the Declaration also considers as refugee persons who have fled their country because their lives, security or liberty have been threatened by generalized violence, foreign aggression, internal conflicts, massive violations of human rights or other circumstances which have seriously affected public order."

However, the Cartagena Declaration taken the individual's need for international protection and, in particular,, the need to protect the physical integrity of the person as the starting point for developing the refugee definition; it is the right to life, security and liberty of a person including the right not to be subjected to arbitrary arrest or detention or to torture as defined in international law which are protected rights.

Although the Cartagena Declaration is not a legally binding instrument -for States, it is nevertheless Of fundamental importance as it reflects consensus on particular principles and criteria and has guided states in their treatment of refugees for the last five years. In fact, & Declaration revitalized the tradition of asylum in Latin America while aiming at consolidating a regional custom for the treatment of refugees, returnees and displaced, persons.

**Refugees in Municipal Laws**

The conventional obligation to protect political refugees is undertaken by a large number of countries. However, the obligation-to protect humanitarian refugees is still moral and humanitarian for a large number of countries. In some cases, the principle of asylum for refugees is expressly acknowledged in the constitution. In others, ratification of the 1951 Convention and the 1967 Protocol may have directed effect in local law, while in still other cases, ratifying states may follow up their acceptance of international, obligations by the enactment of specific refugee legislation or by the adoption of appropriate administrative procedures/For example, the definition of refugee in the 1951 Convention and Protocol has been incorporated into the domestic laws of Denmark, France, Germany, Norway and Sweden. The United States and the United Kingdom have based parts of their immigration laws on these instruments.

The institution of asylum in the West is in serious crisis.-" The number of asylum seekers has over-burdened most refugee determination systems in developed countries, undermining their effectiveness, putting in doubt their procedural fairness and objectivity, and prompting many governments to consider the revision of their procedures.

Unfortunately, one is bound to recognize that whatever be the international law on this aspect of refugee problems, states will in fact condition their policies by their ideology. They may even acknowledge the existence of the international legal rules just mentioned, while at the same time finding excuses, such as the need to support-freedom or combat communism or fight colonialism in the name of self- - determination, to justify contrary behaviour. So far the United States is concerned, it is mentioned in the *Department of Justice Immigration- and Nationalization Service Regulations on Refugee and Asylum* procedures, that regardless of any convention definition, "before the beginning of each fiscal year, the President determines the number and allocation of refugees who are of special humanitarian concern to the United States and who are to be admitted during the succeeding twelve months. Any alien who believes he/she is a 'refugee' is defined in.... [The Refugees Act, 1980] . . . and is included in a refugee group of special humanitarian concern as designated by the President may apply for admission to the United States" in accordance with the Regulations. For the purpose of the-Act, the term 'refugee' covers persons outside their own country, or if stateless outside the country of last habitual residence, who are unable or unwilling to return because of the fear of persecution on account of religion, nationality, or political belief, and the like-that is to say for reasons mentioned in the 1951 Convention and the Protocol thereto. The Act then provides that the President may, for the same reasons, classify as a refugee any person within his national territory, or, if stateless, his place of habitual residence.

Canada's Immigration Act, 1976, has adopted the definition of the 1951 Convention and has spelled out detailed rules for the determination of refugee status. Here it may be mentioned that Canada is also prepared to grant refugee status to persons who have not left home, but who fear they may be persecuted or because may be described as 'self-induced' refugees by virtue of changing their own Political opinions.

Although the Convention and Protocol are not formally

incorporated in United Kingdom law, the rules adopted for implementation of the 1971 Immigration Act make express reference to the Convention definition in the context of applications for entry, for extensions of stay, and against deportation.

On October 22,1992, the United Kingdom Government published its Asylum and Immigration Appeals Bill. If it enters into force, it will be the first piece of legislation focusing a most exclusively on asylum. However, it has been argued that, in the absence of specific legislation, the U.K. system is simply 'an informal administrative process'.

In Switzerland, a clear distinction is made between Convention refugees and persons having fled from civil war, internal disturbance or famine. The later category of persons does not enjoy any protection against expulsion or deportation. Australia has also admitted a large number of humanitarian refugees under special arrangements. A recent Portuguese law on asylum provides for a grant of asylum to persons not qualifying as refugees under the 1951 Refugee. Convention.

In Asia, there has so far been no such regional initiative, nor virtually any appropriate domestic legislation, except of course that imposing restrictions on unwanted new arrivals. Although the Asian region has a large share of the global refugee problem, there is a low rate of accession among Asian countries to the international refugee instruments-the 1951 Convention and the 1967 Protocol. In addition, although African States have utilized regional arrangements, such as the OAU, to provide coordinated responses and a legal framework for the refugee problems experienced there, the Asian region has not entered into similar regional arrangements till to date.

**Conclusion**

Thus the 1951 United Nations Refugee Convention was the culmination of an important historical development in the definition or the international plane of basic minimum legal standards for the treatment of refugees. It also constituted a beacon for the future. The adoption of a conceptual definition of the 'refugee' in the convention-definition which is essentially the same as that in the UNHCR Statute-was regarded as a major step forward, compared with the definitions by categories in the Pre-war refugee instruments and in the constitution of the International Refugee Organization. Until recently this definition was readily accepted as a basis for identifying those refugees who were to be benefited from international protection and assistance.

It is now being said that today's refugees are very difficult from the refugees of 1951. Mrs. Sadako Ogata, the UN High Commissioner for Refugees observed that

> "The context in which refugee problem rise these days is becoming increasingly complex. Tremendous migratory pressures have emerged, provoking large movements of people between countries in the South, the South to the North, and from the East to the West, Even the concept who is a refugee requires new clarification."

The definition of the term 'refugee' given by the UNHCR Statute or 1951 Convention has led some to consider that these definitions are essentially applicable to individuals and are of little relevance for today's refugee problem, which are primarily problems of refugee groups. Because, a prima facie group determination of refugee character does not mean that each and every member of the group would satisfy the test of well-founded fear of persecution, if his or her case were individually determined. Group determination by its nature concentrates on the objective situation in the country of origin. However, in order to deal with these new refugee situations the High Commissioner, with the approval of the General Assembly, developed and applied the 'good offices' procedure. This procedure was originally employed to, with respect to refugees outside the competence of the United Nations, specifically, the Chinese refugees in Hong Kong and Tibetan refugees in India, for whom the High Commissioner was called upon to act in a limited manner, namely, for the transmission of contributions. Thereafter, in the new refugee situations in Africa, the 'good offices' concept was used to enable High Commissioner to assist refugee groups under his regular programme. In making this *prima facie* determination of refugee character, the High Commissioner used broad criteria based on the objective situations existing in the country of origin.

Here it may be noted that, the 1951 Convention was primarily by Europeans about Europeans. A frequent criticism of the document is that it is too 'Euro-Centric'. Yet Western Europe now appears among the least committed of the regions to the original humanitarian under pinnings of the Convention. This is evidenced by the restrictive interpretations of controlling legal norms adopted by Government sectors, the implementation of harsh deterrent measures, and reduced financial support for international refugee aid programme. The restrictive attitudes and practices of Western European and North American nations make it unlikely that international agreement can be reached on a new, broader, definition of refugee.

There are many perspectives on the issue of exactly who merits protection under international refuge law. Some argue that the 1951 Convention refugee definition is too rigid to encompass all those fleeing to the west in need of protection and, therefore, that various other categories, such as de fecto or 'humanitarian' refugees, are required. Others believe that the definition is sufficiently elastic, and that it can be applied in such a way as to provide international protection to those who need it. In resolving the problem of who is a Convention refugee in Western countries, a two-fold approach is called for. First, more specific criteria must be developed, in order to eliminate the ambiguities of the Convention definition as far as possible. Second, and most importantly, the Convention definition must be applied uniformly.

However, an agreement on a more precise definition by Western States would ameliorate a number of other serious problems, including the substantial variations in acceptance rates among States, the over-legalization of many refugee determination procedures; and the diverging perceptions of evolving concepts of refugee law, the importance of which was foreseen by the drafters of the 1951 Convention."

To sum up, it may be noted that the convention may not provide an answer to many of today's problems which have a bearing on the Refugee situation. But it should not be a reason for questioning its basic value in the sphere for which it was intended. The Convention should not be blamed for failing to resolve problems with which it was never supposed to deal. It should never be forgotten that the Convention is an essential part of our humanitarian heritage for the international protection of refugees."

# 4

# STATELESSNESS

> "Suppose a half dozen of us are seated around the walls of a very dark room. We are told that somewhere in the open middle space is a chair. Who would find it? Not those of us who sat still and philosophized about where chairs are placed in rooms. The fellow who would locate it is the one who'd get up, then walk and stumble around until he discovered it. Nobody ever found any-thing while sitting down. So, Q.E.D., don't be afraid to stumble."
>
> —*Charles F. Kettering*

'Everyone has the right to a nationality. No one shall be arbitrarily deprived of his nationality, nor denied the right to change his nationality." Such is the pronouncement of Article 15 of the 1948 Universal Declaration of Human Rights. The right to a nationality and the need to ensure realization of an effective nationality, of a nationality acting as a basis for the exercise of other rights, have been developed through the course of this century. This may be noted in the 1930 Hague Convention on Certain Questions Relating to the Conflict of Nationality Laws promulgated under the auspices of the League of Nations following *World War I,* and the 1961 Convention on the Reduction of Statelessness promulgated under the auspices of the United Nations following World War II. The principles in these conventions have been elaborated upon and reinforced by other landmark conventions, court jurisprudence and State practice. The fight to a nationality is a basic human right acting as a premise for resolution of any issues or questions pertaining to nationality.

Given that everyone has the right to a nationality, how is this right to be realized, how is nationality to be ascribed? International law stipulates that it is for each State to determine, by operation of internal law, who are its citizens. This determination should, however, accord with general principles of international law and, in particular, with principles relating to the acquisition, loss, or denial of citizenship. The codification of principles relating to nationality in international instruments such as the Universal Declaration has been a major development in international law.

Despite significant developments in international law and practice relating to nationality, however, the international -community currently faces numerous situations of Statelessness and the inability to establish a nationality. The problem has arisen in connection with State succession and the adoption of nationality legislation by new or restored States, but is also seen In areas of the world which have had no recent change in legislation and have undergone no transfer of territory. Those affected include life-long residents of a State, ethnic minorities, and in some cases women and children who are rendered stateless because their husband or father is stateless.

The emergence of conflicts involving ethnic groups, numerous sudden cases of State succession, and increased displacement have brought the nationality issue to the foreground. The international community is, as a consequence, turning to international instruments which reflect developments, made in international law and were structured to resolve problems such as those which have arisen. The 1954 Convention relating to the Status of Stateless Persons and the 1961 Convention on the Reduction of Statelessness, developed under the auspices of the United Nations, serve as the reference points for international consensus on principles relating to the problem of statelessness.

Nationality, and the ability to exercise the rights inherent in nationality, act as stabilizing factors and aid in the prevention of involuntary movements between States. Hence, the 1954 Convention relating to the Status of Stateless Persons and the 1961 Convention on the Reduction of Statelessness have taken on new relevance and political significance. 'Orphan" conventions which, until recently, have not been actively promoted due to the lack of a supervisory body or other mechanism which might disseminate them, the 1954 and 1961 Conventions are now tools by which the international community can seek to address emerging and weighty problems relating to nationality.

UNHCR has been approached by both individuals and Governments seeking advice and assistance in nationality matters, including in the drafting and implementation of nationality legislation. An essential step in strengthening efforts to reduce statelessness and the inability to establish nationality, is securing accession to international instruments which ensure, as a minimum: that persons will not arbitrarily be deprived of nationality-, that they will be granted a nationality under certain circumstances in which they might otherwise be stateless; and that adequate protection will be available to those who, nonetheless, remain or become stateless.

Accession to the 1954 Convention relating to the Status

of Stateless Persons is important because it provides stateless individuals with many of the rights necessary to live a stable life. Accession to the 1961 Convention on the Reduction of Statelessness would, moreover, serve to resolve many of the situations which result in statelessness. The 1961 Convention, embodying principles already generally accepted under international law, is a useful 'reference point for nationality legislation and can help resolve certain conflict of laws problems, thereby indicating the international community's resolve to reduce statelessness. An increase in accession to and ratification of these international instruments would act, therefore, as an impetus for all States to work toward the reduction, and eventual elimination, of statelessness.

Due to recent developments, statelessness, although not a new phenomenon, has taken on new dimensions. Its potential as a source of regional tension and of involuntary displacement has come to be more widely recognised. The General Assembly of the United Nations and the Executive Committee of the High Commissioner's Programme have respectively adopted resolutions and conclusions stressing the importance of the principles embodied in these instruments, and the need for States to adopt measures to avoid statelessness. The ability to exercise an effective nationality and the prevention and reduction of statelessness are a contribution to the promotion of human fights and fundamental freedoms, to the security of peoples, and to stability in international relations. UNHCR is pleased to provide this Accession Package in furtherance of these goals.

Historically, there has been a recognized link between Refugees and stateless persons with both groups receiving protection and assistance from international Refugee organizations.

In the wake of world war two when the needs of Refugees were paramount the 1951 Refugee convention was promulgated. A Statelessness protocol, attached to the draft Refugees conventions, was postponed for consideration at a later date.

This protocol was made a convention in its own right in 1954 and UNHCR has been requested by its Executive committee and the UN General Assembly to promote accession to and implementation of the 1954 convention in all states.

Additionally UNHCR has been asked by the General Assembly, under Article 11 of the 1961 convention on the reduction of Statelessness to help individuals and states to resolve cases of Statelessness.

Now the question arise—how do people become stateless?

People can become stateless through:

(i) the transfer of territory or sovereignty which alters the nationality status of citizens of the former State(s) and may leave some persons stateless.

(ii) arbitrary deprivation of nationality or denationalization of groups or individuals by the State.

(iii) conflicts of laws (for example, when a child is born in a State that grants nationality by descent only but the laws of the State of which the parents are nationals grant nationality by birth on their territory only).

(iv) administrative or procedural problems, such as excessive fees, Unrealistic deadlines, lack of appeal or review procedures, failure to notify individuals of registration or other obligations, or unattainable documentation or criteria for confirming or obtaining nationality.

(v) individual renunciation of nationality without prior acquisition, or guarantee of acquisition, of another nationality.

(vi) marriage or the dissolution of marriage, if nationality is automatically lost as a result (women are most at risk of becoming stateless in these cases).

(vii) failure to register children at birth so they cannot show where or to whom they were born (as nationality is normally granted based on where a child is born or based on descent from nationals, failure to register births can easily result in statelessness).

(viii) discriminatory practices based upon ethnicity, religion, gender, race, or political opinion when granting or denying nationality.

(ix) birth to a stateless person.

**Developments in International Law**

Nationality, or citizenship, has been described as man's basic night, as, in fact, the fight to have rights. When viewed in this fight, two aspects of citizenship become apparent, the first being that citizenship is a right, and the second being that the realization of this fight is a necessary precursor to access to other rights. Nationality provides the legal connection between an individual and a State which serves as a basis for certain rights, including the State's fight to grant diplomatic protection and representation of the individual on the international level. The exercise of an effective nationality is, further, a stabilizing and connecting factor, decreasing the potential for population movement or displacement. General Assembly Resolution 50/ 152 of 9

February 1996, calls upon States 'to adopt nationality legislation with a view to reducing statelessness, consistent with fundamental principles of international law." While the extension of certain fights generally associated with nationality, such as voting, employment, or ownership of property, may be one means of normalising the status of non-citizens on a State's territory, there is no replacement for nationality itself

As early as 1923, the Permanent Court of International Justice (PCIJ), in its *Advisory Opinion on the Tunis and Morocco Nationality Decrees,* stated:

> "The question whether a certain matter is or is not solely within the domestic jurisdiction of a State is an essentially relative question; it depends on the development of international relations".

Thus, while nationality issues were in principle within domestic jurisdiction, the PCIJ pointed to restrictions, governed by rules of international law, made incumbent on State discretion by obligations undertaken towards other States.

This theme was woven into the 1930 Hague Convention on Certain Questions Relating to the Conflict of Nationality Laws. Held under the auspices of the Assembly of the League of Nations and the first international attempt to ensure that all persons have a nationality, the Hague Convention picks up this theme and goes further. Article I states:

> "It is for each State to determine under its own law who are its nationals. This law shall be recognised by other States in so far as it is consistent with international conventions, international custom, and the principles of law generally recognised with regard to nationality".

This reference to the three primary sources of international law, later encoded in Article 38 of the Statute of the International Court of Justice, is important. When a State takes action to determine who its nationals or citizens are, this determination should accord with the relevant provisions of international law. As international law develops over time, developments in the field of nationality and statelessness should be taken into consideration by States when they determine nationality status for persons under their jurisdiction.

The term "genuine and effective link" was first enunciated in the Nottebohm Case as a means of defining the nature of nationality. The International Court of Justice (ICJ) stated:

> "According to the practice of States, to arbitral and judicial decisions and to the opinion of writers, nationality is a legal bond having as its basis a social fact of attachment, a genuine connection of existence, interest and sentiments, together with the existence of reciprocal rights and duties".

The genuine and effective fink, as extrapolated from the Nottebohm Case, has since been developed into a broader notion in the area of nationality, as based upon principles embodied in State practice, treaties and case law. For purposes of nationality determination, such factors as birth on a State's territory and/or descent from nationals have been determined to constitute a significant link in the avoidance of statelessness, as has long-term residency and other connecting factors between an individual and a State. These factors are reflected in the nationality legislation of many States.

Human rights principles are also relevant to the problem of statelessness and should be considered by States in assessment of nationality determination. Article 15 of the 1948 Universal Declaration of Human Rights declares:

> "Everyone has the right to a nationality. No one shall be arbitrarily deprived of his nationality nor denied the right to change his nationality".

It should, further, be recalled that the bulk of human rights law has developed in the years following the decisions of the PCIJ and ICJ, and the promulgation of the Hague Convention and the 1961 Convention itself. Article 5 of the International Convention on the Elimination of All Forms of Racial Discrimination seeks, with respect to the right to nationality:

> "To prohibit and to eliminate racial discrimination in all its forms and to guarantee the right of everyone, without distinction as to race, colour, or nationality or ethnic origin, to equality-before the law".

In addition to the 1961. Convention on the Reduction of Statelessness, other international legal instruments dealing with the right to a nationality include the. 1957 Convention on the Nationality of Married Women, the 1966 Covenant on Civil and Political Rights, the 1979 Convention on the Elimination of All Forms of Discrimination Against Women, and the 1989 Convention on the Rights of the Child. The 1957 and 1979 Conventions seek to grant women equal rights with men to acquire, change, or retain their nationality. The husband's nationality status should not automatically change the nationality of the wife, render her stateless, nor mandate acquisition by her of his nationality.

Under the 1979 Convention on the Elimination of All Forms of Discrimination Against Women, women should also have equal rights with men with respect to the nationality of their children, avoiding both discrimination against women and the inheritance, where applicable, of the father's statelessness. The 1989 Convention on the Rights of the Child stipulates that children should be registered immediately after birth, a crucial factor in establishing both place of birth and descent for purposes of acquiring nationality. Children have the right, from birth, to acquire nationality, as provided for in both the 1989 Convention and the 1966 International Covenant on Civil and Political Rights. Convention on Human Rights, stating:

Reference may also be made to regional instruments, such as the 1969 American convention on Human Rights, starting :

> "Every person has the right to a nationality. Every person has the right to the nationality of the State in whose territory he was born if he does not have the right to any other nationality. No one shall be arbitrarily deprived of his nationality or of the right to change it".

These principles have been supported by the jurisprudence of the Inter-American Court. Further, while it has confirmed that the conditions under which nationality will be conferred remain within the domestic jurisdiction of the State, the Court stated in an Advisory Opinion:

> "Despite the fact that it is traditionally accepted that the conferral and recognition of nationality are matters for each State to decide, contemporary developments indicate that international law does impose certain limits on the broad powers enjoyed by the States in that area and that the manner in which States regulate matters bearing on nationality cannot today be deemed to be within their sole jurisdiction"."

The 1997 European Convention on Nationality, promulgated under the auspices of the Council of Europe, is a valuable reference point for general consensus on nationality issues and developments for the forty member States participating in its elaboration. The Convention stipulates that-account should be taken of the legitimate interests of States and of individuals with reference to nationality. The avoidance of statelessness, the right to a nationality for all, and a prohibition concerning discriminatory distinctions are principles underlying all provisions of the Convention. Provisions of the 1961 Convention on the Reduction of Statelessness are incorporated into the 1997 European Convention as regards the grant of nationality to a child born on a State's territory or descended from a State's national in instances where statelessness would otherwise result.

With these developments in international law in the field of nationality, the 1961 Convention on the Reduction of Statelessness may be seen consolidating principles of equality, non-discrimination, protection of ethnic minorities, rights of children, territorial integrity, the right to a nationality and the avoidance of statelessness. The 1961 Convention does not require a contracting State unconditionally to grant nationality to any stateless persons but seeks, rather, to balance factors of birth or descent in an effort to avoid the creation of statelessness. Procedural guarantees are also required to avoid the creation of statelessness through an inadvertent loss of nationality. This approach is developing as a principle in international law outside the context of the 1961 Convention on the Reduction of Statelessness.

**UNHCR and Statelessness**

UNHCR has always had responsibilities for stateless refugees, under its statutory function of providing international protection as well as under the 1951 Convention relating to the Status of Refugees. In recent years, furthermore, the Office has been encouraged to seek preventive action by addressing the causes leading to involuntary displacement. Clearly, the realization of an effective nationality and the ability to realise the rights inherent in nationality act as stabilizing factors in the prevention of involuntary and coerced movements between States.

There is a fink between the loss or denial of national protection and the loss or denial of nationality. On the plane of rights, the prevention and reduction of statelessness is an important aspect of securing minority rights. While the basic human rights of stateless persons are, in principle, to be respected in the country of habitual residence, it is clear that there are stateless persons who may not receive the national protection necessary for a stable life.

The prevention and reduction of statelessness and the protection of stateless persons are important for the prevention of potential refugee situations. UNHCR has been entrusted by the General Assembly with fulfilling the functions foreseen under Article 11 of the 1961 Convention on the Reduction of Statelessness. When the 1961 Convention was to enter into force, UNHCR was asked provisionally to assume the responsibilities foreseen under Article 11 'of a body to which a person claiming the benefit of this Convention may apply for the examination of his claim and for assistance in presenting it to the appropriate authority". As the agency designated to act as an intermediary between States and stateless persons under the 1961 Convention, it is incumbent upon UNHCR to provide expertise in the area of nationality legislation to States parties.

The principles embodied in the 1961 Convention have served as a reference point for determination of international law and international consensus regarding nationality and have been incorporated into numerous treaties and international instruments; as well as into national legislation.

Thus, while there are a minimal number of States signatory to the 1961 Convention, the general principles embodied in the Convention are inherent in nationality legislation and practice in many States, and have served as a means of ascertaining consensus on legal standards to be applied in the area' of nationality to problems of statelessness. These standards include the avoidance of statelessness and the grant of nationality to those who have an effective link or appropriate connection with the State.

Of further relevance to UNHCR's interactions with States on questions pertaining to nationality is the Conclusion on The Prevention and Reduction of Statelessness and the Protection of Stateless Persons, adopted by the High Commissioner's Executive Committee and endorsed by United Nations General Assembly Resolution 50/152 of 9 February 1996. The General Assembly encouraged the High Commissioner to continue her activities on behalf of stateless persons, as part of her statutory function of providing international protection and of seeking preventive action, as well as her responsibilities under General Assembly Resolutions 3274 (XXIV) of 10 December 1974 and 31/36 of 30 November 1976, and now:

> "Requests the Office of the High Commissioner, in view of the limited number of States party to these instruments, actively to promote accession to the 1954 Convention relating to the Status of Stateless Persons and the 1961 Convention on the Reduction of Statelessness, as well as to provide relevant technical and advisory services pertaining to the preparation and implementation of nationality legislation to interested States;

> Calls upon States to adopt nationality legislation with a view to reducing statelessness, consistent with fundamental principles of international law, in particular by preventing arbitrary deprivation of nationality, and by eliminating provisions which permit the renunciation of a nationality without the prior possession or acquisition of another nationality, while at the same time recognising the right of States to establish laws governing the acquisition, renunciation or loss of nationality".

To this end, UNHCR has provided advice and assistance to governments and individuals in nationality matters, including in the drafting and implementation of nationality legislation. The Office will continue to provide technical and advisory services and to promote the statelessness Conventions as part of its responsibility under Article 11 of the 1961 Convention, as well as in response to the request of its Executive Committee to 'provide relevant technical and advisory services pertaining to the preparation and implementation of nationality legislation".

UNHCR is concerned with nationality legislation which could lead to displacement. In its Resolution of 1996, the General Assembly expressed its concern that 'statelessness, including the inability to establish one's nationality, may result in displacement" Lack of an effective nationality including national protection is also relevant and there are numerous cases in which de facto statelessness has been shown to be connected to population displacement. While some refugees are *de jure* stateless, many refugees are de facto stateless, making this category, or its potential creation, of great concern to the Office.

When the 1954 and 1961 Conventions were drafted, it was assumed that all de facto stateless persons were refugees and would, therefore, benefit from the 1951 Convention. It is now apparent that there are those who do not qualify as refugees but whose nationality status is unclear. The situation of such a person in terms of a lack of national protection may be identical to that of a *de jure* stateless person. Since lack of protection may result in involuntary displacement, UNHCR is also concerned with promotional and preventive measures on behalf of such individuals. UNHCR continues to explore promotional and preventive activities in this area to which the Office can contribute in collaboration with concerned States.

# 5

# Asylum for Refugees

> "There is sometimes as much ability in knowing how to profit by good advice as in arriving at a correct opinion ourselves."
>
> —*Francois De La Rochefoucauld*

The concept of asylum is an ancient one going back to the sanctuary rented to those who, against political or even criminal prosecution, sought refuge in a place of, religious devotion. During the Middle Ages and the formative stages of international law up to the end of the nineteenth century, asylum was frequently granted by one State to the enemies of another usually because the granting State disapproved of the political or religious intolerance of the State fled.

Britain, for example, had virtually an open door policy to the victims of persecution, and for that reason was antipathetic to the, idea of 'concluding extradition treaties with other countries, even limited to ordinary criminals, until very late in the nineteenth century.The concept of asylum has undergone a significant change in the twentieth century. The United Nations Charter again and again, stresses faith in fundamental human rights' and 'promoting and encouraging respect for human rights and fundamental freedoms' for all without distinction as to race, sex, language or religion.

The Universal Declaration of Human Rights, adopted by the UN General Assembly in 1948, stated in Article 14(1) that-

> "everyone has the right to seek and enjoy in other countries asylum from persecution".

Here it is interesting to note that no definition of the term persecution' was offered, thus leaving the matter entirely to the discretion of the host State of judge and no corresponding duty was laid on states to grant asylum.'

Like the 1951 Convention on Refugees, the 1967 Declaration on Territorial Asylum does not seek to impose on states an obligation to grant territorial asylum to any person qualified to seek it. What the Declaration essentially does is to emphasize the rule of non-refoulement. Article 30 states that-

> "no person shall be subjected to measure such as rejection at the frontier or, if he has already entered the territory in which he seeks asylum expulsion or Compulsory return to any State where he may be subjected to persecution".

Article 33 of the 1951 Convention also lays down the principle of non-refoulement by stating that-

(1) No contracting state shall expel or return a refugee in any manner whatsoever to the frontiers of territories where his life or freedom ' would be threatened on account of his race, religion, nationality, membership of a particular social group or political opinion.

(2) The benefit of the present provision may not however, be claimed by a refugee whom there are reasonable grounds for regarding as a danger to the security of the country in which he is, or who, having been convicted by a final judgement of a particularly

serious crime, constitutes a danger to the community of that country.

The Committee on the Enforcement of Human Rights Law of the International Law Association-in its report for the Buenos Aires Conference held in August 1994 stated, inter alia, that despite widespread acceptance of the 1951 Convention on the Status of Refugees and the 1967 Protocol thereto, the right set forth in Art. 14 of the Universal Declaration has not been identified by commentators or states 'as falling within customary international law; however, returning a person to a country where he would be, tortured might well violate a developing customary norm against the refoulement of refugees . So, the central problem to be addressed is the legal status of the right to seek and enjoy asylum in general and the principle of non-refoulement in particular.

The international community has reacted to the asylum crisis inter alia by trying alternative methods of improving the legal framework of territorial asylum. Within United Nations this has been done mainly through the Executive Committee of the High Commissioner's Programme. The UNHCR Executive Committee has adopted significant conclusions on asylum and non-refoulement, particularly at its twenty-eighth, thirtieth and thirty-first sessions in October 1977, 1979 and 1980 respectively. One of the conclusions "reaffirms the fundamental importance of the principle of non-refoulement both at the border and within the territory of a state of persons i who may be subjected to persecution if returned to their country of origin irrespective of whether or not they have been formally recognized as refugees".

**United Nations Conference on Territorial Asylum**

In view of the General Assembly Resolution 3456 (XXX)

of December 9, 1975, delegates of 92 countries met at a Conference in Geneva from January 10 to February 4, 1977. The task of the Conference was to adopt the Convention on Territorial Asylum, working on the basis of the draft convention draw up in May 1975 by a group of experts (convoked by the United Nations General Assembly). But, due to highly diverse stands taken by individual delegations, the conference failed to agree on the text of the new Convention. In view of this situation, the delegations deferred further consideration of the proposed new convention to an indefinite date.

However, today, the generally accepted position would appear to be as follows: states consistently refuse to accept binding obligations to grant to persons any rights to asylum in the sense of a permanent right to settle. Apart from any limitations which might be imposed by specific treaties, states have been adament in maintaining that the question of whether or not a right of entry should be afforded to an individual or to a group of individuals, is something which falls to each nation to resolve for itself. Anyway, non-refoulement has not become a rule of general customary international law", although there are some disputes both as to the existence of any binding rule, and as to its exact ambit.

So far as the practice of the states is concerned, it undoubtedly indicates that they have been very generous in granting asylum, not only to individuals, but also in the case of mass influx. The most recent example of this is the decision of the Bhutan Government not to give effect to its earlier decision to repatriate 400 Tibetan refugees who refused to accept Bhutanese citizenship, because of the common religion of Tibet and Bhutan and also because Bhutan is a Member of the United Nations."

**Temporary Asylum**

During the cold war, asylum tended to be linked either to permanent settlement in the country where refuge was first sought or to resettlement in another country. At the time, safe return was not viewed, among western governments, as a realistic possibility for refugees—coming from most communist countries. The provisions of the 1951 Convention that relate to the economic and social rights of refugees were therefore seen as tools to promote their integration in the country of asylum. But, today, the opportunities for permanent integration in receiving countries are limited, It seems very unlikely that people who have fled *en-masse* to a neighbouring country will in the future be offered large-scale resettlement elsewhere, as happened in the case of the Vietnamese boat people in the 1980s and that of the Hungarian three decades earlier.

Most asylum countries in the developing world suffer from increasing pressure on land and water resources. Local integration is correspondingly less practical, both in economic and political terms. So, these countries do not view asylum on their territory as permanent but as a temporary and pragmatic response to humanitarian emergencies offered until such time as refugees feel safe to go home voluntarily. Western governments, too, are increasingly resorting to temporary asylum.

However, during the past 15 years millions of refugees have been admitted to countries on a temporary basis. Many remained there for months, even years, and only a few were granted refugee status or the rights usually accorded to alien residents. The often precarious situation of people given temporary asylum is aggravated by the lack of a definite legal status to protect them. As there is no provision in the 1951 Convention which can satisfactorily be applied to this category, except to describe them as "refugees unlawfully in the country of refuge" (Art. 31), and as they can not remain indefinitely in that condition, the experts thought that basic minimum standards should be formulated to save them from arbitrary treatment. So, the fundamental rule of protection, non-refoulement of persons to frontiers of territories where their life would be threatened, has to be retained. Further, their safety, and their right to care and maintenance, should be assured, and they should not be penalised for their entry into, or presence, in, the country. They should also not be submitted to inhuman treatment, or measures of discrimination, and the unity of the family should be respected.

Finally, despite controversy over many issues, the 171 countries which are parties to *1993 Vienna Declaration on Human Rights* reaffirmed 'their commitment to the purposes and principles contained in the Charter of the United Nations and the Universal Declaration of Human Rights' and also emphasized that the Declaration "is the source of inspiration and has been the basis for the United Nations in making advances in standard setting as contained in the existing human rights instruments'. Moreover, the Vienna Conference stresses the importance of the right to seek and enjoy asylum as a normative provision of the Universal Declaration; prohibition against torture being considered another such normative provision.

**Refugees Status**

Once the asylum-seeker has been admitted to the country of refuge, and the danger of persecution thereby averted, the inevitable question of his rights and duties arises, According to customary international law, the asylum-seeker's status is chiefly governed by the fact that he now falls under the territorial jurisdiction of the receiving State Generally speaking, he occupies the position of any normal alien, with the proviso that he may not be expelled to his home country unless there are grave reasons for doing so.

As an alien, the refugee is entitled to treatment in accordance with the rule of law, as well as to the benefits of the "minimum treatment rule. The refugee can not claim rights not otherwise granted by legislation to foreigners, such as permission to work, assistance under public or social schemes etc. In addition, he has to submit to the rules pertaining to alien administration.

General international law is silent on the question of the political rights of refugees in their country of residence. The attitude of some states is stricter in this matter than others. It would seem that, in general, refugees have no right to engage in political activities going beyond the normal freedoms, such as freedom of speech, conscience, etc. On the contrary, states may incur international responsibility if they allow or Support the activities of exiles directed against the government of another State. It remains a moot point in how far the country of nationally remains entitled to protect, or to enforce its laws against, a refugee who has fled abroad. Under customary international law, nationals abroad remain under the supremacy of their home-state, and according to the rules of conflict of laws, their personal status is governed by the country of either nationality or legal domicile.

This means in effect that unless the country of asylum, in the exercise of its rights to afford refugee, adopts special provisions regulating his status and legal capacity, the refugee may find himself in difficult circumstances. The law is indeed vague on this point, and all depends on the arrangements made by the individual States.

The 1951 Convention relating to the Status of Refugees

lists the principle rights which the contracting states undertake to grant them, subject to exceptions relate to each country's particular requirements. Interesting from both a juridical and a political point of view is, first, the international nature of the status afforded to persons qualifying under Article I of the Convention. They have been officially released to a large extent from their attachments to their country of origin, and placed under an internationally guaranteed protection, and this under the supervision of a United Nations organ, the Office of the High Commissioner for Refugees. Secondly, the treatment of refugees is enhanced far above that of ordinary aliens."'

The 1951 Convention establishes three standards of treatment as regards specific rights of refugees:

(1) National treatment, i.e., the same treatment as is accorded to nationals of 'the contracting state concerned;

(2) Most favoured nations treatment, i.e. the most favourable treatment accorded to nationals of a foreign country; and

(3) "treatment as favourable as possible, and in any event not less favourable than that accorded to aliens generally in the same circumstances".

According to 1951 Convention refugees are to be given the same treatment as nationals in respect to certain basic rights, such as freedom of religion, access to court's, possession of property, as well as in matters pertaining to public relief rationing and elementary education. Subject to certain qualifications, national treatment is also granted in wage-earning employment, labour and social security legislation. The personal status of refugees is to be governed by the laws of the country of asylum, and they are to be exempted from exceptional measures. Moreover, after three years' residence, exemption from legislative reciprocity is ensured.

Most-favoured nation treatment is to be accorded to refugees in respect of permission to create and join non-political and non-profit-making associations and trade unions, as well as in matters relating to the right, to engage in wage-earning employment for those who have not yet fulfilled the requirements for national treatment.

"Treatment as favourable as possible and, in any event, not less favourable than that accorded to aliens generally" is granted as regards the aquisition and lease of property, the right to engage in agriculture, trades, handicrafts or business, and to practice a liberal profession. Matters such as housing, higher education and related subjects are regulated in a similar manner.

However, among the main rights of concern to the refugee is that of free access to employment, which in practice means that right to an independent existence. In the case of wage earning employment, Art. 17 of the Convention provides that the contracting state shall accord to refugees lawfully staying in their territory the most favourable treatment accorded to aliens. In addition to this general principle there are special provisions in favour of refugees who have completed three years' residence in the country, or whose children or spouse possess the nationality of that country. The latter are exempted from any restrictive measures imposed on aliens for the protection of the national labour market.

So far the freedom of movement is concerned-Art. 26 of the Convention proclaims the rights of refugees to choose their place of residence and to move freely within the territory of the country concerned. Although the principle of the free choice of place of residence is very widely accepted, its application is sometimes hampered by the regulations on access to employment. The OAU. Convention provides that refugees shall, as far as possible, be settled at a reasonable distance from the frontier of their country of origin,

**Travel Documents for Refugees**

Unlike an ordinary alien, a refugee does not enjoy the protection of the country of his nationality and can not therefore avail himself of a national passport for travel purposes. When the international community, after World War I, approached the task of establishing an internationally recognised status for refugees, one of the first measures taken was to ensure that refugees were provided with documentation to enable them to travel. The form and content of this documentation varied at different times, but provided the basis from which the "Convention Travel Document" developed.

The Convention Travel Document is now regularly issued by States parties to the 1951 Convention or to the 1967 Protocol relating to the Status of Refugees and is also widely recognised by States which are not parties to these instruments.

Article 28 of the 1951 Convention provides that:

1. The Contracting states shall issue to refugees, lawfully staying in their territory travel documents for the purposes of travel outside their territory unless compelling reasons of national security or public order otherwise require, and the provisions of the schedule to this convention shall apply with respect to such documents. The Contracting States may issue such a travel document to any other refugee in their territory; they shall in particular give sympathetic consideration to the issue of such a travel document

to refugees in their territory who are unable to obtain a travel document from the country of their lawful residence.

2. Travel documents issued to refugees under previous international agreements by parties thereto shall be recognized and treated by the Contracting States in the same way as if they had been issued pursuant to this article."

An obligation to issue travel documents in accordance with this article is also assumed by States upon becoming parties to the 1967 Protocol relating to the Status of Refugees.

Here it may be noted that/an exception to the requirement that contracting states issue travel documents to refugees lawfully staying in their territory is to be found in the words "unless compelling reasons of national security or public order otherwise require". So, not every case which would ordinarily fall under the latter concept would therefore justify a refusal of travel document, but only reasons of a very serious character.

In the 1969 OAU Convention, there are no provisions relating directly to the rights of refugees granted lawful residence. This was because, as the preamble to the convention makes clear, the 1951 Convention constitutes "the basic and universal instrument relating to the Status of refugees". As the 1969 OAU Convention was designed to complement and supplement the 1951 Convention, it was not considered necessary to add to the 1969 OAU Convention provisions relating to the rights of refugees granted lawful residence.

The 1966 Bankok Principles contain a provision on minimum standard of treatment. Article VI states:

1. A state shall accord to refugees treatment in no way

less favourable than that generally accorded to aliens in similar circumstances.

2. The standard of treatment referred to the preceding clause shall include the rights relating to aliens contained in the Final Report of the Committee on the Status of aliens, annexed to these principles, to the extent that they are applicable to refugees.
3. A refugee shall not be denied any rights on the ground that he does not fulfil requirements which by their nature a refugee is incapable of fulfilling.
4. A refugee shall not be denied by right on the ground that there is no reciprocity in regard to the grant of such rights between the receiving state and the state or country of nationally of the refugee or, if he is stateless, the state or country of his former habitual residence.

**Right of Family Re-unification**

A refugee may be granted all the normal rights of lawful residence but if he is separated from his spouse, children or parents, he may endure acute -'suffering. To his isolation is added the pain of the loss of the society of his family. The right to family re-unification is derived from the basic principle of human rights stated-in Art. 16(3) of the 1948 Universal Declaration of Human Rights:

> "The family is the natural and fundamental group unit of society and is entitled to protection by society and the State"

Unfortunately, none of the existing international legal instruments on asylum or the protection of refugees contain a provision on family re-unification.

The Final Act of the 1951 Convention of the Status of Refugees contained a recommendations stating:

"The Conference:

Considering that the unity of the family, the national and fundamental group unit of society, is an essential right of the refugees, and that such unity is constantly threatened, and noting with satisfaction that.... the rights granted to a refugee are extended to members of his family;

Recommends Governments to take the necessary, measures for the protection of the refugees' family, with a view to:

(i) that the unity of the refugees' family is maintained particularly in cases where the head of the family has fulfilled the necessary conditions for admissions to a particular country; and

(ii) the protection of refugees who are minors, in particular unaccompanied children and girls, with special references to guardianship and adoption".

Here it may be noted that the Executive Committee of the United Nations High Commissioner for Refugees, at its twenty-eighth Session in 1978, adopted a conclusion on family reunion which :

(a) reiterated the fundamental importance of the principle of family reunion;

(b) reaffirmed the co-ordinating role of UNHCR with a view to promoting the reunion of separated refugee families through appropriate intervention with Governments and with inter-governmental and non-governmental organizations:"

Farther, in 1981, recognizing the necessity of the minimum standards of treatment of asylum-seekers who have been temporarily admitted to a country pending arrangements for a durable solution, the Executive Committee of the UNHCR Programme adopted all these basic standard of treatment of refugees as described above.

Needless, to say, the interpretation and application of the 1951 Refugee Convention are left first and foremost, with the contracting states. Its previsions become national law, and the asylum-seeker is thereby placed in a position to claim his rights before thę competent municipal authorities and tribunals. However, the international community, in particular the United Nations, has aimed higher in its attempts to provide an international standard of treatment of refugees. By a series of General Assembly Resolutions, the world's; refugees were formally placed under the protection of international society as a whole.

Prince Sadruddin Aga Khan, the former United Nations High Commissioner for Refugees, has rightly observed:

> "A rule of the law can not be judged solely by its actual wording and purport; everything depends on how it is applied. This fact has been confirmed by the UNHCR's own day-to-day experience in performing its protection function. Its efforts to persuade governments to make their internal legislation more favourable and equitable for refugees therefore have to be accompanied by constant vigilance, to ensure that a rule which has been adopted is not evaded, wrongly interpreted or simply ignored. This applies particularly, and above all, in such vital areas as the grant of asylum..... Hence the great importance, in the country of reception, of the presence of a UNHCR representative who can know the details of particular cases and who can intervene before it is too late".

# 6

# Refugee Problem: A Socio-political Analysis

> "The very core of peace and love is imagination. All altruism springs from putting yourself in the other person's place."
>
> —*Harry Emerson Foskick*

Refugee law exists in order to interpose the protection of the international community in situations where resort to national protection is not possible. Because it is fundamentally a form of surrogate or substitute protection, the beneficiaries of refugee law have always been defined to exclude those who enjoy the basic entitlements of membership in a national community, and who ought reasonably to vindicate their basic human rights against their own state. Refugees are unprotected persons, not just in the sense that their basic liberties or entitlements are in jeopardy, but more fundamentally because it is impossible for them to work within or even to restructure the national community, of which they are nominally a part in order to exercise those human rights. Their position within the home community is not just precarious; there is also an element of fundamental marginalization which distinguishes them from other persons at risk of serious harm. As stated by Rogers Smith:

> The refugee has been cast adrift, usually because his religion, ethnicity, economic aspirations, political beliefs or political alliances in some way stand opposed to his putative government's efforts to create and sustain a strong nation state.

The early refugee accords did not articulate this notion of disfranchisement or breakdown of basic membership rights, since refugees were defined simply by specific national, political, and religious categories, including anti-Communist Russians, Turkish Armenians, Jews from Germany, and others. The *de facto* uniting criterion, however, was the shared marginalization of the groups in their states Of origin, with consequent inability to vindicate their basic human rights at home. These early refugees were not merely suffering persons, but were moreover persons whose position was fundamentally at odds with the power structure in their home state. It was the lack of a meaningful stake in the governance of their own society which distinguished them from others, and which gave legitimacy to their desire to seek protection abroad.

The modern refugee definition gave voice to this premise by moving away from protection on the basis of named, marginalized groups, and toward a more generic formulation of the membership principle. Given the prevailing primacy of the civil and political paradigm of human rights, it was contextually logical that marginalization should be defined by reference to norms of non-discrimination; a refugee was defined as a person at risk of serious harm for reasons of race, religion, nationality, membership of a particular social group, or political opinion. The rationale for this limitation was not that other persons were less at risk, but was rather that, at least in the context of the historical moment, persons affected by these forms of fundamental' socio-political disfranchisement were less likely to be in a position to seek effective redress from within the state.

The particular historical context which led to the linkage between refugeehood and civil or political status notwithstanding, the analysis which follows will show that it is largely possible for a liberal interpretation of the five enumerated grounds to sustain the Convention's vitality. By contouring the bases for claim so as to identify instances of fundamental disfranchisement in which deference to national remedies for human rights violations is not viable, refugee law can remain meaningful to the modern victims of socio-political marginalization.

## Race

The first form of disfranchisement within the scope of refugee law is that based on race. While the drafters of the Convention did not specifically define the term, the historical context makes clear that their intent was to include those Jewish victims of Naziism who had been persecuted because of their ethnicity, whether or not they actively practised their religion. This historical rationale is important, because it legitimizes the attribution of a broad social meaning to the term "race" which includes all persons of identifiable ethnicity.

As Atle Grahl-Madsen has observed, the Convention's notion of race includes not only persons at risk by reason of their membership in a particular scientific category, but also other groups such as Jews and Gypsies whose physical or cultural distinctiveness has caused them to suffer social prejudice. The possibility of overlap between race and other enumerated factors such as religion, nationality, and membership of a particular social group is thus clear, but presents no real problem since claims may be based on one or a combination of forms of civil or political disfranchisement.

A broad interpretation of race is not only historically defensible, but is moreover consistent with modern international usage. The widely accepted International Convention on the Elimination of All Forms of Racial Discrimination, for example, defines "racial discrimination" as including differential treatment based on "race, colour, descent, or national or ethnic origin". In the refugee context, the clear majority of delegates to the Conference on Territorial Asylum similarly agreed to extend protection to persons persecuted for reasons of "race, colour, national or ethnic origin". The Executive Committee of the UNHCR adopted this perspective, and has recommended a comprehensive definition of race to states:

> Race, in the present connexion, has to be understood in its widest sense to include all kinds of ethnic groups that are referred to as "races" in common usage. Frequently, it will entail membership of a specific social group of common descent forming a minority within a larger population.

This UNHCR-derived interpretation has been explicitly adopted into Canadian law in a series of decisions commencing with Boleslaw Dytlow, as well as in immigration policy guidelines. The relevant case law has equated race with "ethnic background", "heritage", and "distinct minority" status. Among those whose claims have been dealt with on the basis of race are Ibos from Nigeria, the Mohajirs of Pakistan, the Baganda from Uganda, Guyanese of East Indian descent, Tamils from Sri Lanka, the Baluba from Zaire, and Gypsies of Polish origin. The primary notion which unites these groups is their exclusion from state protection based on identifiable ethnicity.

The equation of race with minority status must be viewed in the context of effective political power, not just numbers. Since refugee law is concerned with the absence of protection rather than with minority status *per se,* the members of a country's ethnic majority may be protected as racially defined refugees if they are disfranchised in terms of respect for core human rights. In Pierre Katanku Tshiabu Tshibola, for example, the Immigration Appeal Board accepted the claim of a Baluba from Zaire. It noted that while the Baluba constitute half the population of that state, the Ngwandi ethnic group holds effective power, thereby creating a risk of oppression for the Baluba. Similarly, in the case of Ganganee Janet Permanand the Board observed:

> The Indo-Guyanese community to which the claimant belongs is the largest in number in Guyana. The numerical majority, of course, does not necessarily guarantee immunity from persecution by a minority holding the power of the State.

One can similarly imagine the extension of this principle to blacks in South Africa, and to other ethnic groups denied effective political voice within their country of origin. Majority status alone does not negate a claim to racially defined refugee status if discernible ethnicity gives rise to a genuine risk of serious harm not remediable by national protection.

### Nationality

Closely linked to the notion of race or ethnicity is the concept of nationality. As in the case of race, the drafting history of the Convention offers no specific definition of nationality. The early commentators assumed a narrow meaning of the term, roughly equivalent to formal citizenship, leading to the obvious question of why a state would choose to persecute its own citizens merely by reason of their status as citizens. A slightly more expansive interpretation of citizenship, however, suggests a number of situations in which disfranchisement on the basis of formal political status is conceivable.

First, resident internationality unprotected persons, such as refugees and stateless persons, might be the objects of human rights abuse by reason of their status as "foreigners". While inhabitants who retain the formal and effective citizenship of another state could not advance a claim to refugee status in relation to the state of domicile, those who cannot enjoy meaningful protection elsewhere are properly assessed as refugees -in accordance with the concept of state of former habitual residence. Second, persons who are denied full citizenship in their own state (such as Palestinians in Israel) could qualify as nationally defined refugees in sofar as their inferior political status can be shown to put them at risk of persecution. Third, some states may disfranchise a portion of their population by ascribing a different nationality to them (as in the case of the black "homelands" in South Africa), and establishing regimes which fail to guarantee basic human rights to those assigned the new "nationality". Fourth, persecution based on nationality might arise in the context of a state composed of previously sovereign territories (such as the U.S.S.R.), where measures are directed against those who define their nationality in terms of allegiance to the predecessor state.

In addition to notions of formal nationality, it is generally suggested that nationality encompasses linguistic groups and other culturally defined collectivities, thus overlapping to a significant extent with the concept of race. Because many such groups share a sense of political community distinct from that of the nation state, their .claims to refugee protection may reasonably be determined on the basis of nationality as well as on race.

**Religion**

Religion as defined in international law consists of two elements. First, individuals have the right to hold or not to hold any form of theistic, nontheistic, or atheistic belief. This decision is entirely personal: neither the state nor its official or unofficial agents may interfere with an individual's right to adhere to or to refuse a belief system' nor with a decision to change one's beliefs. Second, an individual's right to religion implies the ability to live in accordance with a chosen belief, including participation in or abstention from formal worship and other religious acts, "pression of views, and the ordering of personal behaviour.

Because religion encompasses both the belief that one may choose to hold and behaviour which stems from those beliefs, religion as a ground for refugee status similarly includes two dimensions. First is the protection of persons who are in serious jeopardy because they are identified as adherents of a particular religion. It is not necessary that a claimant have taken any kind of active role in the promotion of her beliefs, nor even that she be particularly observant of its precepts or rituals. In the case of Francisco Jorge/Carvalho Penha, for example, the Immigration Appeal Board remarked that " [t]he fact that [the claimant] had not received baptism does not detract from the . . . claim since he was perceived by members of his community as being a Jehovah's Witness." This decision contrasts favourably with other cases in which protection on the ground of religion was limited to objectively defined religious practitioners. The central issue must be whether there is a linkage between the threat of persecution and the claimant's self-defined or externally ascribed religious beliefs, in which case refugee protection is warranted.

Alternatively, because religion includes also behaviour which flows from belief, it is appropriate to recognize as refugees persons at risk for choosing to live their convictions. This proposition is constrained only by the limitation , expressed in the International Covenant on Civil and Political Rights:

> Freedom to manifest one's religion or beliefs may be subject only to such limitations as are prescribed by law and are necessary to protect public safety, order, health, or morals or the fundamental rights and freedoms of others.

While the scope of this restriction is arguably broad, the assertion in one Board decision that "[g]iven the applicant's religious attitude ... one might reasonably expect that he will 'keep his mouth shut'" is simply wrong. The peaceful expression of one's beliefs, including engaging in worship, playing an active role in religious affairs, and proselytizing may give rise to a genuine need for protection. Religious behaviour includes more than just formal acts of worship, and may encompass, for example, conscientious objection to military service.

The notion of persecution on account of political opinion was conceived in liberal terms. The Convention's drafters noted that in addition to "diplomats thrown out of office" and persons "whose political party had been outlawed", even "individuals who fled from revolutions" ought to be encompassed by the political opinion category. That is, protection on the ground of political opinion was to be extended not only to those with identifiable political affiliations or roles, but also to other persons at risk from political forces within their home community. Contemporary Canadian jurisprudence mirrors this historical conceptualization in most respects.

Because the Convention definition refers to "political

opinion" rather than to the arguably more constrained notion of "political activity", there is no requirement that a claimant have acted upon her beliefs prior to departure from her country in order to qualify for refugee status. As stated in the landmark decision of *Juan Alejandro Araya Heredio:*

> . . . the Convention speaks not of political activities but of political opinions. Opinions are often, but not necessarily, expressed in action, and history has taught us that some political regimes... persist in pursuing some of their nationals simply because the latter supported a former regime or collaborated with it, or simply because they oppose or, owing to their former loyalties, constitute a challenge to the authority now in power.

In some circumstances, the expression of a non-conforming political belief while in the home state may simply have been a practical impossibility, while in other cases the applicant may not have held or felt as strongly about the particular belief at the time of departure. Because the refugee definition requires a forward-looking assessment of risk, the issue to be addressed is whether there is reason to believe that the claimant's decision to exercise her right to form an opinion "on any matter in which the machinery of state, government, and Policy may be engaged" Would place her in jeopardy upon return to her home state.

### Membership of a Particular Social Group

The fifth enumerated ground for persecution, membership of a particular social group, was introduced with little explanation by the Swedish delegate as a last minute amendment to the Refugee Convention:

> ... experience had shown that certain refugees had been persecuted because they belonged to particular social

> groups.... Such cases existed, and it would be as well to mention them explicitly.

Who were the intended beneficiaries of this provision? On the one hand, it is argued that membership of a particular social group should be seen as "clarifying certain elements in the more traditional grounds for persecution", those being race, religion, nationality, and political opinion. This was Canadian practice for some years, resulting in the recognition of social group claims only when the social group could be defined on the basis of one of the other four forms of civil or political status:

> Either the group must be political and proclaim and exhibit dissidence with the regime or be a religious sect which has been persecuted by the civil authorities because of its religious beliefs. In a multinational state, a racial minority might also constitute such a group.

Under this approach, the notion of membership of a particular social group became largely superfluous, since the groups which were recognized - illegal expatriates, human rights activists, and various anti-government associations - could already be protected under the rubric of one of the other four categories. The inappropriateness of this neutering of the social group criterion was noted by the Federal Court of Appeal in Attorney General of Canada v. Patrick Francis Ward.

> It was the contention of counsel for the Respondent that any reasonably definable organization engaged in political activity may be included in the definition [of a particular social group). If that were so, I find it difficult to understand why it was necessary to include in the definition the term "a particular social group" when the term "political opinion" is part of the definition.

Alternatively, the plea has been made to interpret membership of a particular social group as an essentially all-embracing "safety net", requiring only some recognizable similarly of background among group members. The position is most forcefully put by Arthur Helion, who argues:

> The delegates intended to guarantee security from persecution to all refugees, without invidious or unnecessary distinctions. The "social group'; category, designed to reaffirm this commitment, was adopted in the U.N. Convention without dissent, extending the protection of refugees far beyond what had previously been the norm.... The intent of the framers of the Refugee Convention was not to address prior persecution of social groups, but rather to save individuals from future injustice. The "social group" category was meant to be a catch-all which could include all the bases for and types of persecution which an imaginative despot might conjure up.

Helton goes on to suggest that all groups protected under any U.N. human rights convention, whether defined in statistical, societal, social, or associational terms, should be considered within the scope of the Convention.

The notion of social group as an all-encompassing residual category is seductive from a humanitarian perspective, since it largely eliminates the need to consider the issue of a linkage between fear of persecution and civil or political status. Yet this is precisely the reason that Helton's analysis cannot stand. The drafters of the Convention did not wish to avoid drawing distinctions among various types of putative refugees, but rather intended to establish a demarcation between those whose fear was attributable to civil or political status (refugees) and those whose concern to flee was prompted by other concerns (not refugees). Moreover, their purpose was anything but the creation of a regime to address new, future injustices, as Helton suggests. It is clear from the comments of the Swedish proponent of the social group category and others that the Convention was designed simply as a means of identifying and protecting refugees from known forms of harm, not of anticipating future, distinct types of state abuse. The liberal attempt to give life to the notion of social group has therefore gone too far, effectively disregarding the fourth element of the Convention definition. This trend has nonetheless been endorsed in some Canadian case law, including in recent comments of the Federal Court of Appeal which seem to define a particular social group simply as a group of persons "associated, allied, combined" and "united in a stable association with common purposes", with the possible caveat that its goals must not challenge "democratically constituted authority".

**Gender**

Gender-based groups are clear examples of social subsets defined by an innate and immutable characteristic. Thus, while gender is not an independent enumerated ground for Convention protection, it is properly within the ambit of the social group category. The Executive Committee of the UNHCR endorsed this approach in its 1985 conclusion on "Refugee Women and International Protection":

> . . . States, in the exercise of their sovereignty, are free to adopt the interpretation that women asylum-seekers who face harsh or inhumane treatment due to their having transgressed the social mores of the society in which they live may be considered as a "particular social group" within the meaning of Article I(A)(2) of the 1951 United Nations Refugee Convention.

The decision in *Zekiye Incirciyan* offered the first clear indication that Canadian law would follow the international lead. This case involved a Turkish widow, who had no close family in that country. She was harassed on a daily basis by young men, was sexually assaulted, and was the object of an abduction attempt. The Immigration Appeal Board found that the government was unwilling to protect the claimant because, in the authorities' view, it was inappropriate for her to be living without the protection of a male relative. Accordingly, the Board determined Mrs. Incirciyan to be a refugee by reason of her membership of a particular social group composed of "single women living in a Moslem country without the protection of a male relative." This category meets the test for a particular social group, since gender and the absence of male relatives are not within the control of group members, and choice of marital status is a freedom guaranteed under core norms of international human rights law.

Early decisions of the Immigration and Refugee Board have similarly recognized the appropriateness of the social group designation for women in Lebanon and for Tamil women in Sri Lanka. Men, too, have occasionally benefitted from gender-specific interpretations of the social group category, as in Oscar *Roberto Cruz* where the Board noted that the Salvadoran claimant was "a young man, a member of the broad social group that is the primary target of military and guerrilla alike". While some have expressed reservations about the broad ambit of gender-defined social groups, adherence to the *ejusdem generis* principle defeats such concerns, since race, nationality, religion, and even political opinion are also traits which are shared by large numbers of people.

**Sexual Orientation**

Homosexual and bisexual women and men constitute a second group defined by a fundamental, immutable characteristic. The Federal Administrative Court of Germany addressed the potential for homosexuality to define a "particular social group" in a 1986 decision involving the alleged persecution of an Iranian male by reason of his sexual orientation.

Noting the persecution of homosexuals in the Nazi concentration camps, the Court recognized the viability of considering sexual orientation as the basis for a claim to refugee status, assuming it to be an irreversible personal characteristic. While the precise issue has not yet been adjudicated in Canada, the basis for treating sexual orientation as an immutable characteristic capable of defining a social group was established by the decision of the Federal Court Trial Division in *Timothy Veysey v. Commissioner of the Correctional Service of Canada.*

The applicant in that case alleged a breach of his right to equality by reason of the refusal of prison officials to extend the conjugal visitation policy in force for heterosexual spouses to include also homosexual spouses. In finding a violation of the equality rights provision of the Charter of Rights and Freedoms, Mr. Justice Dube applied the ejusdem generis test to define the scope of non-enumerated heads of equality. His conclusions are unmistakably pertinent to the definition of "particular social group" in refugee law:

> Most of the grounds enumerated in s. 15 of the Charter as prohibited grounds of discrimination connote the attribute of immutability, such as race, national or ethnic origin, colour, age. One's religion may be changed, but with some difficulty; sex and mental or physical disability, with even greater difficulty. Presumably, sexual orientation would fit within one of these levels of immutability. Another characteristic common to the enumerated grounds is that the individuals or groups involved have been victimized

> and stigmatized throughout history because of prejudice, mostly based on fear or ignorance, as most prejudices are. This characteristic would also clearly apply to sexual orientation, or more precisely to those who have deviated, from accepted sexual norms, at least in the eyes of the majority.

**Family**

In view of the recognition in international law of the family as "the natural and fundamental group unit of society [which] is entitled to protection by society and the State", it is not surprising that refugee claims based on family affiliation have been recognized as within the scope of the social group category, both in Canada and elsewhere. Indeed, one of the few provisions which delegates to the unsuccessful Conference on Territorial Asylum were able to agree upon was the inclusion of "kinship" as a proper basis for the recognition of refugee status. The first Canadian decision to raise the possibility that one's family might constitute a particular social group within the meaning of the Convention definition was the 1979 judgment of the Federal Court of Appeal in *Astudillo V. Minister of Employment and Immigration.*

There followed a series of judgments of the Immigration Appeal Board which impliedly accepted this premise by recognizing the claims of siblings and children of activities, as well as those made by members of politically prominent families more generally. It was not until the case of Richard Cid Requena Cruz, however, that family was clearly stated to be a part of the concept of particular social group. In response to the petition of a young Peruvian who was the object of police harassment in consequence of the escape from the country of his father, the Board observed:

> The application, based on social group, raises the question as to whether or not a family can be

> considered a social group for the purposes of the Immigration Act, 1976. The answer to that question is a qualified yes. In some cultures, including Latin America, certain African nations and some others, for example, it is quite likely that an individual will be assumed to be a supporter of specific social, religious or political ideas merely because a father, uncle or other prominent family member is a known advocate of those ideas. This is not always so, however, and each case must be decided on its own merits on the basis of evidence presented.

The *Requena Cruz* doctrine has been applied in a variety of circumstances, including the claims of the wife of a Chilean socialist, the cousin of an opponent of the Guyanese government, and the son of the organizer of a coup in Ghana. As a rule, therefore , whenever there is an indication that the status or activity of a claimant's relative is the basis for a risk of persecution, a claim grounded in family background is properly receivable under the social group category. Moreover, as the decision in Maria Mabel de la Barra Velasquez Suggests, the notion of family is culturally relative, and may extend significantly beyond nuclear and blood relationships.

**Class or Caste**

A fourth form of particular social group encompasses immutable forms of class and caste. While it is often suggested that notions of class and social group are essentially coterminous, the general definition posited above excludes a social class defined by a changeable characteristic of a non-essential nature. For example, the members of a privileged social class who resist renunciation of economic privilege are not protected, since it is within their ability voluntarily to renounce their property, an interest which is not protected under core human rights norms.

The exclusion would not apply, however, if the members of the privileged, class were forever stigmatized for their origins even after renouncing their property, since past status is an immutable characteristic. In the case of *Luis Folhadeld Carneiro de Oliveira,* for example, the Board examined the claim of a Portuguese millionaire industrialist whose vast holdings had been nationalized and confiscated by the government which came to power in 1974. While this fact alone ought not to constitute the basis for a refugee claim, the Board was of the view that the claimant's fear of reprisals for his *past* social status, including the possibility of arrest without trial, was sufficient to bring him within the definition of membership of a particular social group.

Similarly, an economic class is within the scope of a particular social group where membership, though nominally voluntary, is the only means of ensuring basic subsistence, an interest protected under core norms of human rights law. In the case *of Joseph Alexis Manasse,* the Immigration Appeal Board correctly held membership in the Haitian peasant landowning class to be a form of particular social group, since in the context of a poor, agrarian society, membership in the class represents a means of access to basic needs. The central question, therefore, in examining wealth-based categories or classes is whether the group's defining characteristic is either innate or unchangeable, or if subject to voluntary alienation, whether it is premised on the realization of basic human rights. In all other cases, it would be reasonable to expect an applicant to accommodate herself to less privileged circumstances as an alternative to the invocation of international protection.

**Voluntary Associations**

Perhaps the most contentious aspect of the social group concept relates to membership in associations from which voluntary alienation is possible. Normally, the social group designation is concerned with the protection of persons from abuse based on characteristics which are beyond their control - gender, sexual orientation, family, and most forms of class or caste. However, as the decision in *Matter of Acosta* suggests, immutability should be interpreted to include "a characteristic that either is beyond the power of an individual to change or *is so fundamental to individual identity or conscience that it ought not be required to be changed.* "[Emphasis added]

Thus, membership in a voluntary association defined by a non-fundamental purpose, such as recreation or personal convenience, would normally be seen to be outside the scope of the notion of a particular social group. Conversely, where the purpose of the voluntary association is essential to individual identity or conscience, it is reasonable that members should have access to international protection -where there is a risk of persecution for failure to renounce such basic interests. This approach- is consistent with the decision of the Federal Court of Appeal in *Attorney General of Canada v. Patrick Francis Ward,* in which an attempt was made to define the social group concept as applied to voluntary associations by examining the legal acceptability of their goals.

Students are thus logically included within the social group category, since the pursuit of education is a basic international human right. This characterization was raised as a possibility by the Federal Court of Appeal's decision in *Gladys Maribel Hernandez,"* and has been adopted by the Immigration Appeal Board in *Jesus Antonio Miranda Cuellar.* More generally, groups defined by employment or profession fall within the social group category, since freedom to choose one's occupation is also a basic right. Trade union membership has also been accepted as the basis for refugee status in decisions such as *Wilfredo Alejandro Zubieta* and Oscar *Trujillo*

*Barraza.* In all of these examples, voluntary participation is appropriately protected because of its linkage to core principles of human rights. The interests which underlie membership in the associations are so fundamental that international protection is in keeping with the underlying rationale for the social group category.

**Criminal' Status: Prosecution or Persecution?**

It is clear that refugee status may not be invoked by an individual solely on the basis that she is at risk of legitimate prosecution or punishment for breach of the ordinary criminal law. As the UNHCR has noted:

> Persecution must be distinguished from punishment for a common law offence. Persons fleeing from prosecution or punishment for such an offence are not normally refugees. It should be recalled that a refugee is a victim - or potential victim - of injustice, not a fugitive from, justice.

This proposition was propounded as part of Canadian law in the decision of *Louis-Paul Mingot,* in which it was held that "[f]ear of being legally prosecuted before regular courts... [cannot] in se and per se, constitute a fear of persecution as defined in the Convention". This is so even if the justice system in the country of origin fails to meet generalized standards of fairness, or the range of penalties ordinarily imposed in that nation seems out of line with the norms in other states. The case of Ghanaian *Anthony Appiah Asamoah,* for example, raised the issue of an individual at risk of prosecution under very stringent laws for having allowed fire to destroy another's crops, who claimed refugee status on the basis of the in appropriateness of summary prosecution and severe penalties for offences of this kind. In rejecting his claim, the Board noted:

> ... he has shown that he fears prosecution for an economic offence in Ghana, an offence which indeed may carry severe penalties with it and may not proceed entirely in accordance with Canada's criminal justice and evidentiary rules... [but] this offence is not directed solely against the applicant himself, but rather is applied to the population of Ghana in general. How this can be characterized as persecution is a question which has not been answered ....

Such claims are outside the scope of the Convention because the risk faced by the claimant is only the potential criminal liability of every citizen, and is therefore not linked to a form of civil or political status enumerated in the definition. Insofar as an examination of both the nature of the criminal offence and its prosecution and punishment confirms that the offence is politically neutral in substance and application, then it cannot serve as the basis for a claim to refugee status.

On the other hand, Richard Plender has observed that while persecution and prosecution are not coterminous, neither are they mutually exclusive.", Because both the content and implementation of the criminal law are within the control of the state of origin, it is possible for a government with persecutory intent to use the criminal law as a means of oppressing its opponents. In such circumstances, it makes no sense to treat those at risk of politically inspired abuse of the criminal law as fugitives from justice; they are rather potentially at risk of persecution, and may property be assessed as refugees.

This perspective is consistent with the internal structure of the Convention, the exclusion clauses of which deny refugee status not, to all "criminals" *per se,* but only to a person who "has committed a serious *non-political* crime outside the country of refuge. . ." [Emphasis added]. Similarly, the Draft Convention on Territorial Asylum provides for a clarification of the refugee definition to embrace persons at risk of prosecution or punishment for reasons directly related to. .. persecution".

Canadian law has only recently begun to examine critically the context of alleged criminality in a comprehensive way. In *Ethem Ictensev,* the Board posed the question,

> When is a political action permissible although forbidden by law? Clearly, for our purposes, the fact that a political action is taken outside of the law is in itself not sufficient to invalidate a claim. However, the question posed cannot be answered in a simplistic fashion, for it involves the consideration of a large number of issues ranging from human rights to state security; from natural justice to emergency measures.

A turning point was reached in the decision of Ghanaian *Godfred Appiah Kubi,* involving an individual charged with the "criminal offence" of distributing anti-government pamphlets. After conducting a thorough review of the conflicting Canadian jurisprudence, the Board concluded that ". . . the commission of an offence should not automatically lead to the conclusion that the claimant's fear is of prosecution and punishment". Looking beyond the alleged illegality of the act, the Board in this case noted that" [distributing pamphlets is often the only means of expressing contrary opinions in countries where there are restrictions on freedom of expression, a fundamental human right," and accordingly determined the criminal characterization of the claimant's actions to be without foundation.

**Refusal to Perform Military Service**

Persons who claim refugee status on the basis of a

refusal to perform military service are neither refugees *per se* nor excluded from protection. In general terms:

> A person is clearly not a refugee if his only reason for desertion or draft-evasion is his dislike of military service or fear of combat. He may, however, be a refugee his desertion or evasion of military service is concomitant with other relevant motives for leaving or remaining outside his country, or if he otherwise has reasons, within the meaning of the definition, to fear persecution.

In this sense, the determination of a refugee claim grounded in refusal to perform military service is comparable to the issue of criminality just examined: the crucial question is whether the claimant can show that desertion or evasion is grounded in civil or political status, tailing which the claim cannot succeed.

The insufficiency of a non-specific desire to escape a military service obligation is established by cases such as Tadeusz Adamusik, in which the Immigration Appeal Board dismissed the claim of a Polish draft evader, noting simply that " [t]o serve in the armed forces is a duty of all Polish citizens and, therefore, the Board cannot consider Mr. Adamusik to be a refugee just for this reason". This general position is derived from the notion, noted in *Victor Fathy Kamel,* that "The Convention does not contain any sections dealing [specifically] with army deserters or conscientious objectors". Simply put, the nexus between the harm feared and civil or political status is absent.

The first exception to the exclusion of military evasion and desertion from the scope of the Convention involves claims based on the fact that conscription for engagement in a legitimate and lawful purpose is conducted in a discriminatory manner, or that prosecution or punishment for evasion or desertion is biased in relation to one of the five Convention-based grounds of protection. This is essentially the parallel of the distortion of the general criminal law for a discriminatory purpose discussed above: where a form of state-sanctioned harm is inflicted through the subversion of an otherwise lawful system, the differential nature of the risk based on discriminatory administration may remove the claim from the realm of ordinary military conscription. Where, for example, only members of a particular racial group are subject to conscription, where the military service obligation is enforted more rigorously against persons of a particular political perspective, or where the penalty for evasion or desertion is applied differently to members of a given religious group, the refugee claim should be fully examined on its merits. A second qualification to this rule arises when desertion or evasion reflects an implied political opinion as to the fundamental illegitimacy in international law of the form of military service avoided.

As Gilbert Jaeger writes,

> ... a broad perception in democratic countries is that there is considerable difference between military service by consent, instituted according to democratic legislative process and called upon to defend the life of a democratic society, on the one hand, and on the other hand, military service in a dictatorial or quasi-dictatorial regime railed upon to defend institutions and policies unrelated to accepted human' rights standards or, even worse, utilized for internal or external aggression.... [T]he right to refuse military service on account of its illegitimate political purpose... is formally acknowledged by the UN General Assembly; such refusal qualifies an individual for the grant of asylum and refugee status.

As in the case of an absolute political offence, 301 there is a range of military activity which is simply never permissible, in that it violates basic international standards. This includes military action intended to violate basic human rights, ventures in breach of the Geneva Convention standards for the conduct of war, and non-defensive incursions into foreign territory. Where an individual refuses to perform military service which offends fundamental standards of this sort, "punishment for desertion or draft evasion could, in the light of all other requirements of the definition, in itself be regarded as persecution".

This exception has been specifically recognized by the General Assembly of the United Nations in its Resolution 33/165, dealing with the status of persons refusing service in military or police forces used to enforce apartheid in South Africa. Because such service is inherently violative of basic human rights, the General Assembly agreed to call upon states to

> ... grant asylum or safe transit to another State, in the spirit of the Declaration on Territorial Asylum, to persons compelled to leave their country of nationality solely because of a conscientious objection to assisting in the enforcement of apartheid through service in military or police forces; [and urged] Member States to consider favourably the granting to such persons of all the rights and benefits accorded to refugees under existing legal instruments ....

## Victims of War and Violence

While the Refugee Convention was conceived as a response to the victims of war, it was not intended that all those displaced by violent conflict should enjoy refugee status:

> The text ... obviously did not refer to refugees from natural disasters, for it was difficult to imagine that

> fires, flood, earthquakes or volcanic eruptions, for instance, differentiated between their victims on the grounds of race, religion, or political opinion. Nor did the text cover all man-made events. There was no provision, for example, for refugees fleeing from hostilities unless they were otherwise covered by Article I of the Convention. [Emphasis added]

This extract from the drafting history of the Convention makes clear two essential points. First, victims of war and conflict are not refugees unless they are subject to differential victimization based on civil or political status." Second, it follows that it is incumbent on decision-makers to examine the claims of persons in flight from violence in order to ascertain whether their particular circumstances disclose any evidence of a link between the harm feared and their civil or political status.

Concern about the inappropriateness of this selective approach to the protection of war refugees has led to the drafting of regional standards in both Africa and Latin America which provide for the general enfranchisement of the victims of violence. UNHCR has provided assistance to the victims of war, and it *is* arguable that a customary norm of providing temporary refuge to the victims of generalized violence is evolving from the practice of states. Nonetheless, the Convention today remains firmly anchored in the notion of elevating only a subset of those at risk of war and violent conflict to the status of refugee.

This-general proposition is well -established in Canadian law by a variety of cases involving the victims of violence in Lebanon Ethiopia, and Chile. Moreover, as the decision in Elias Iskantlar Ishac makes clear, the mere fact that the conflict escaped is based on religion or politics is not relevant unless persons of a particular religion or political perspective are differentially at risk. In this case, the Board found the risk to be roughly equivalent for persons of all beliefs, and hence refused the claim of a citizen of Lebanon attempting to escape the civil war in that country:

> If the appellant is a refugee at all, he is a refugee from civil war in his country, and not a refugee protected by the Convention. ... A civil war, even on religious grounds, is not persecution as contemplated by the Convention.

This general rule, however, admits of two important exceptions.

First, persons may be differentially at risk where the civil war or violence is directed at a particular social subgroup. This principle derives from the decision in Tekeste Kifletsion, in which an Eritrean from Ethiopia was determined to be a Convention refugee on the basis of the genocidal conflict directed against members of his race by the Ethiopian government:

> ... a civil war against a minority race inside a country, verging on genocide, is without doubt evidence of racial persecution.

Here, it could not truly be said that the claimant was at risk only of an undifferentiated harm affecting all members of his society, but was rather specifically at risk by reason of his race. This exception was affirmed by the Board in *Adan Jeronimo Alvarenga:*

> Civil war in itself does not constitute persecution as contemplated by the Convention; however, a civil war directed against a religious group in particular or a social group would be persecution within the definition in the Convention.

Second, even within the context of generalized violence

or war, there may exist a risk of serious harm specific to persons defined by a particular form of civil or political status. While early Canadian decisions preferred simply to adopt an absolutely dismissive view of claims derived from situations of conflict, the decision of the Federal Court of Appeal in *Zahirdeen Rajudeen v. Minister of Employment and Immigration* marked a watershed in the approach to this issue. This case involved a Sri Lankan Tamil whose need for protection from Sinhalese thugs had been ignored by the authorities. The Immigration Appeal Board dismissed the claim as nothing more than a reflection of the generalized violence in Sri Lanka. The Federal Court, however, found that the harm faced by the claimant was in fact due to the unwillingness of authorities to protect him because of his race and religion:

> The applicant was not mistreated because of civil unrest in Sri Lanka but because he was a Tamil and a Muslim.

This decision underscores the critical importance of inquiring into all of the circumstances of a claimant coming from an area which suffers from generalized violence in order to discern whether or not the risk faced by a particular individual or group is in fact rooted in civil or political status, in which case refugee status may follow.

# 7

# Humanitarian Assistance for Refugees

> "America does not consist of groups. A man who thinks of himself as belonging to a particular national group in America has not yet become an American."
>
> —*Woodrow Wilson*

The creation of international machinery to deal with the problem of refugees and, for that matter, international social and humanitarian co-operation, was not envisaged in the Covenant of the League of Nations of 1919. These questions were not then deemed to be of sufficient importance to merit other than general treatment. Yet, at that time, vast number of refugees were already living in desperate circumstances, and were dependent on assistance from private and national sources for the barest necessities of life. Help from international sources was needed to keep them alive. No thought was given, however, to the creation of an international body to tackle all the aspect of a situation which threatened to assume alarming proportions.

When wave upon wave of refugees, began to break over Europe and Asia-Minor from 1915 onwards, the first assistance given to them came from relief societies, the refugees' own mutual aid associations, and a number of organizations set up in certain countries to distribute foreign relief.

In Asia-Minor, from 1915 onwards, various organisations, including the American Red Cross, undertook, on behalf of Armenian refugees, relief operations which were to continue until 1923. In the course of the years 1918 to 1922,1,500,000 persons left Russia to escape the effects of famine and other consequences of war and troubled times, and were assisted in different countries of refugee by various charitable organizations, including the American Red Cross. In March 1923, the American Red Cross was feeding every day more than half-a-million Greek refugees from Anatolia, while the Turkish Red Crescent was one of the organizations helping the Turkish Government to bring relief to Ottoman refugees coming from Greece. As some (if these refugees trickled slowly into Western European countries, they sought, and found, relief and assistance from national Red Cross Societies which helped their integration in their new country of asylum. However, the situation called for energetic and imaginative action.

On February 16,1921, the International Committee of the Red Cross (ICRC) convened to an unofficial meeting in Geneva, representatives of the International Labour Office, the International Union for Helping the Children, the London Save the Children Fund, the League of Red Cross Services, and the Russian relief associations, to consider what action could be taken to alleviate the distress of the various groups of post-World War-I or post-Russian-Revolution refugees, and to coordinate measures of assistance.

However, in the meeting, it was decided to lay the question of Russian refugees before the Members of the League of Nations, and to suggest the appointment of a League of Nations Commissioner to deal with the various aspects of the refugee problem, as it existed at that time; to centralize all refugee relief work; and above all, to provide legal and political protection for refugees. This proposal was warmly welcomed by a number of governments, and the League of Nations decided on June 27,1921 to appoint as High Commissioner for Refugees Dr. Fridtjof Nansen, who had just completed the task of bringing home 400,000 prisoners of War. His mandate was to seek a permanent solution for the refugee problem then in existence, and to co-ordinate the efforts made in various countries by governments and private organizations.

In the exercise of his task, Dr. Nansen enlisted the services of voluntary bodies, calling, in particular, upon the assistance of the ICRC and several of its delegations, including those in Athens, Belgrade, Bucharest, Budapest, Constantinople, Righ and Warsaw. He further established an advisory body of the private relief organizations concerned with Russian refugees among which were the ICRC, the League of Red Cross Societies, and the American Red Cross. For almost nine years, until his death in 1930, Dr. Nansen was the League of Nations High Commissioner for Refugees. Nansen was faced with the need of finding funds for the maintenance of the refugees and offers for their settlement in' other countries. Between 1924 and 1929 the task of material assistance for refugees was entrusted to the International Labour Organization, and Protection functions became the main responsibility of the High Commissioner. In 1929 both tasks were reunited in the Office of the High Commissioner. On the death of Dr. Nansen in 1930, the Nansen International Office for Refugees was created by a resolution of the Assembly of the League of Nations, as an autonomous body responsible for exercising functions, including humanitarian assistance.

The financing of the refugee operation was a continuous problem. The League of Nations paid only for administrative expenses and assumed on the whole no responsibility for the funding of aid for refugees. Funds had to be solicited from Governments, voluntary organizations, and private individuals, largely on an *ad hoc* basis. The Secretariate of the League was entrusted with the protection of the refugees, but this division between political and legal protection on the one hand, and the humanitarian work on the other hand, could not be strictly maintained in practice.

In 1933 a new High Commissioner for Refugee, coming from Germany, was appointed under a mandate excluding any role of assistance. Despite the work of the Nansen Office and the High Commissioner, well over 500,000 refugees in Europe were in urgent need by 1938. In that year the Nansen Office and the Office of the High Commissioner were closed and a new High Commissioner for Refugees under the Protection of the League of Nations was appointed, whose competence relating, to relief was restricted to facilitating the coordination of, humanitarian assistance provided by other organizations.

The Evian Conference of 1938, convened to deal with political and economic questions arising from the exodus of refugees from Germany and Austria, set up the *Inter-Governmental Committee on Refugees (IGCR),* headed by the High Commissioner. However, plans to establish an international organization with responsibility to carry out social, economic and humanitarian functions on behalf of those left in greatest need by the effects of World War-II resulted in the creation of the *United Nations Relief and Rehabilitation Administration (UNRRA)* by 44 nations on November 9, 1943.

UNRRA, established as a specialised agency before the adoption of United Nations Charter and the creation of the

UN itself, was the first major operating agency for refugees and displaced persons. The Administration exercised responsibility for the provision of material assistance to refugees and displaced persons both in Europe and in its other areas of operation, with the participation of over 60 voluntary organizations. UNRRA and IGCR were succeeded, in 1947, by the *International Refugee Organization (IRO).* The IRO's main objective was to achieve voluntary repatriation or resettlement, but it was recognized that immediate maintenance and assistance functions would also be necessary and the Organization was given full power for its tasks of material relief." Between July 1,1947, and January 31,1952 the International Refugee Organization (IRO) succeeded in resettling over one million refugees and it saved hundreds of thousands from starvation by giving them care and maintenance in their countries of residence." The IRO went into liquidation on March 1,1952.

As early as July 1949 it became clear that there would remain a refugee problem after the closure of the International Refugee Organization. The General Council of I.R.O., therefore, addressed a communication to the Economic and Social Council of the United Nations on future international action concerning refugees, in which it came to the conclusion that:

"(a) international assistance in the protection of refugees should continue unbroken;

(b) an organ within the framework of the United Nations should be entrusted with this responsibility; and

(c) the question of the establishment of an international fund for the material assistance of refugees after the termination of the IRO programme should be determined by the Economic and Social Council".

The General Assembly, of the United Nations adopted on December 3,1949, a Resolution to the effect that the international protection of refugees was, as from January 1, 1951, to become the responsibility of a United Nations High Commissioner for Refugees.[15] Thus, the United Nations have assumed direct responsibility for the refugee problem. Here it is worthwhile to mention that the tasks of the IRO were largely operational: care and maintenance, repatriation and resettlement of refugees. On the other hand, the task of the UNHCR is the international protection of refugees and the promotion of permanent solutions for the problem of refugees.

The international response to the plight of refugees is one of the most remarkable humanitarian achievements of the century. Building on foundations laid by, the first High Commissioner for Refugees, *Fridtjof Nansen,* beginning in-1921, the international community has progressively developed the structure and practice of international protection, Elaborating and consolidating a system of legal principles and norms and, most importantly providing asylum to millions of refugees.

The jurisprudential basis of international refugee law is the concept of common humanity and the responsibility of the international community to preserve human life/to promote the well-being of all men, to diminish human sufferings and to assist states in providing protection and assistance to refugees. The protection that the international community extends to refugees must include physical security of refugees, and physical protection also means keeping people alive through humanitarian assistance. Food, water, sanitation and medical care are fundamental to survival. These people walk long distances only as long as their legs can carry them subject to availability of food, water and shelter or until they are stopped. The vast majority of refugee populations live in the immediate vicinity of the only international frontier they have ever crossed-and which they are going to cross again when the time comes for their safe and voluntary return. Only a very few of them have the money, the contacts, the family connections, the knowledge or the inner energy to propel them onwards.

The dependence of growing masses of refugees on organized assistance raises questions as to the extent and capacities of transnational efforts of humanitarian purposes. By the end of 1996 the world's refugee population was estimated by the United Nations High Commissioner for Refugees at some 20 million. Persecution, human rights abuses and civil strife, the major root causes of refugee flows, are increasing, and the complex humanitarian assistance problems generated by the hew conflicts are ever more difficult to resolve.

In the autumn of 1990. United Nations agencies drew up contingency plans for an anticipated flow of refugee from Iraq and Turkey. In April and early May 1991, as government troops closed in, 1.8 million Kurds suddenly headed for the Turkish and Iranian borders. Since then there has been a rapid succession of refugee crisis. In 1992 alone, over 3.5 million people were forced to flee across an international border in search of safety. In the 16 months between December 1991 and June 1993, the number of people dependent on international assistance in the former Yugoslavia rose from 500,000 to 3.6 million. In March 1992, some 3,000 refugees a day were arriving in Kenya to escape the fighting, famine and chaos in Somalia. At about the same time, a quarter of a million Muslim refugees from Myanmar fled into Bangladesh, and up to 500 refugees a day were pouring into Nepal from Bhutan. By late 1992, the conflict between Azerbaijan and Armenia had created more than 800,000 refugees and internally displaced people, while the civil war in, Tajikistan had uprooted another half a million. In February and March, 1993, 280,000 refugees from Togo sought refuge in Benin and Ghana.

More recently, the human tragedy in Rwanda, which resulted in some 200,000 persons killed, more than a million persons becoming refugees in neighbouring Zaire and Tanzania and million others homeless in their own country, is still fresh in the minds of the international community. Millions of Afghan refugees are still unable to return home years after the victory of the Mujahidins because of the infighting among the Mujahidins themselves. Of course, the plight of the Bosnian refugees and the international politics surrounding the conflict has perhaps received, more sustained international attention in the last two years than any other single development. As Peter Macalister-Smith observed:

> "The response to these refugee situations, which were neither envisaged nor provided for in the early Post-war period of international organisation, has included an enlarging of the capacities and functions of the relevant institutions charged with humanitarian tasks. In particular, UNHCR's competence to provide material assistance has been progressively expanded to enable more practical and comprehensive action to be taken to meet the immediate needs of refugees".

For the past several years, ethnic conflict has been the world's most common form of collective violence and a major cause of the steadily increasing refugee problem. Stories of ethnic hatred, xenophobia and racist attacks by neo-Nazi Skin-heads make headlines almost daily in Germany. In Bosnia, rape has been used as weapon of war, to humiliate and destroy Muslim families. Investigators say as many as 20,000 women may have been raped in the brutal conflict in

Bosnia-Herzegovina. Some eyewitness accounts even mention cases of women who are held and repeatedly raped until they become pregnant. They are freed only when it is too late for an abortion. In the view of the perpetrators (in this case the Serbs), the children born of this barbarous union are Serbian.

Thus rape becomes a method of ethnic purification. Here it may be worthwhile to mention that in late 1991, when the United Nation designated the UNHCR as the lead agency for the coordination of humanitarian assistance in the former Yugoslavia, there were some 500,000 refugees and displaced persons in need of assistance as a result of the fighting in the Croatia.

By the end of July 1993, the total population receiving assistance had increased to 3.6 million, with over 2 million in Bosnia-Harzegovina alone. Despite enormous obstacles, the ongoing fighting and the lack of security for relief deliveries, the massive international relief effort is bringing humanitarian relief to millions, with the focus on life-sustaining relief to persons in Bosnia. UNHCR and other UN humanitarian agencies-including UNICEF, WHO and WFP as well as ICRC and large number of NGO's-continue to bring food, medicine and supplies to victims of the war.

Today, several millions of refugees, displaced persons and others whose situation has been considered analogous benefit directly from UNHCR's assistance programmes. UNHCR has also been involved during the post year in a wide -range of activities in favour of internally displaced persons. Ms. Sadako Ogata, United Nations High Commissioner for Refugees, while delivering her address before the Third Committee of the General Assembly on the 10th November, 1992, observed that-

> "The scale and complexity of humanitarian crisis confronting us is a reflection of the uncertainty and instability of the period in which we are living. Resurgent nationalism, coupled with the serious economic and social consequences of the collapse of the old world order, has led to a multiplication of conflicts ...... In such circumstances, my office is faced by a number of fundamental challenges that go to the very heart of its mandate ...... I can not claim to have all answers, Mr. Chairman, but I am confident that, given its unique mandate, its experience, its demonstrated capacity to innovate, and the indispensable support of Governments, my Office will continue to adapt with flexibility and innovation to new challenges while preserving the established principles of international protection"..

However, in the field of international humanitarian assistance, the permanent factor in post-war work for refugees has been the activity of the voluntary agencies. The voluntary agency acts as an intermediary between government and individuals, enabling citizens to coordinate their efforts and achieve a goal. As a channel of good will and positive motivation, the voluntary agency helps to influence governments to establish and carry out comprehensive and humane refugee policy.

Here it is worthwhile to mention that over the decades, the most sustained and devoted service to the cause of refugees has been provided by various inter-governmental organisations and NGOs viz.; UNDP, FAO, WFP, ICRC, ILO, UNICEF,. V OXFAM, ICVA etc. In July 1992, to further enhance emergency-response, the United Nations created the *Department of Humanitarian Affairs (DHA)* with a mandate to co-ordinate UN response in complex humanitarian emergencies.

**The Role of the United Nations Relief and Works Agency for Palestine Refugees in the near East**

The refugees from Palestine who were left in urgent need of humanitarian assistance upon the establishment of Israel as a State, on 14/15 May 1948, continue with their descendants to receive international assistance under the aegis of the United Nations Relief and Works Agency for Palestine Refugees in the Near East (UNRWA). UNRWA was established in 1949 by a resolution of the General Assembly.

The Agency was given two duties : first, to carry out in, collaboration with local governments' the direct relief and works, programmes for the Palestine refugees already recommended, by an Economic Survey Mission; and, secondly, to consult with "interested Near Eastern Governments " about measures to be taken by them against the time when international assistance for relief and works projects would no longer be available. The operations, of the Agency, and the terms of its 'mandate', have been reviewed every year by the Assembly, and resolutions passed accordingly renewing the mandate as required.

From the beginning UNRWA has defined refugees, for the purposes of its mandate, as all persons who had lived in Palestine for at least two years before the Arab-Israel conflict of 1948, and who as a result of it lost both their homes and their means of earning a living; and only these, and their families are qualified for the Agency's assistance as refugees. Refugees wishing for relief have been required to register with the Agency, and there are now over one and a half-million registered refugees. Of these some 187,000 are living in Lebanon, 173,000 in Syria, 5,68,000 in Jordan, 283,000 on the West Bank of the Jordan, and 327,000 in the occupied Gaza Strip. These five countries or territories, together with

Egypt, where there are some 3,000 refugees, form the Agency's area of operations.

The registered refugee is entitled to the assistance available according to his need. This assistance takes four principal forms: rations, housing, medical care and education. One-third of the refugees live in an UNRWA camp. However, the government of the country in which the camp is situated is responsible for law and order therein, and general control and administration. There is in most camps a clinic with a doctor in daily attendance; and for the refugees not living in the camps there are UNRWA clinics or health centres in the major centres of population, and mobile health teams. The Agency has some hospitals of its own. Great attention is paid to sanitation in the camps, and to the provision of drinking water. The Agency, in association with UNESCO, provides free elementary education in its own schools for a period of six years and lower secondary education for a period of three years for those who have satisfactorily completed their elementary education. Altogether the Agency gives education to more than a quarter of a million children. There are also ten institutions for the training of teachers, and for giving training in various trades.

The Secretary-General of the United Nations appoints the Commissioner-General of the agency, and he in turn appoints his staff. However, it is to be mentioned that refugees registered with UNRWA and receiving its assistance are excluded from the competence of the United Nations High Commissioner for Refugees. Since its creation UNRWA has faced continuous budgetary deficits while also experiencing serious difficulties resulting from the armed conflicts in the region. UNRWA's present annual budget is close to $200 million, almost all of which is provided by governments. The largest single contributor is the United States. Other principal contributors are Canada, the Federal Republic of Germany, Japan, Saudi Arabia, Sweden, the United Kingdom and the Commission of the European Communities. As Prof. Jack I. Garvey observed :

> "UNRWA suffers from a continuing and everworsening financial crisis and from political limitations that severely impair its humanitarian function', Nevertheless, UNRWA continues: as an unfavoured stepchild of the United Nations and as a victim of manipulations of Middle East politics"

UNRWA is primarily an operational agency. It controls its own budget from receipt to expenditure. Furthermore, it provides educational, health, and other services in parallel relation to the host government, sometimes intermixing functions with the host, but providing services typically governmental in nature. Of primary significance is the relationship of great mutual dependence between UNRWA and the refugee. For over four decades, UNRWA has responded to the most vital needs of the refugee, on a highly personalized and direct basis, functioning almost wholly through Palestinian staff on the operational level. In the early years, the refugees relied on UNRWA for food and shelter. Today, they rely on UNRWA for the basic security provided by health services and for the refugee family's most tangible hope for the future, the UNRWA education programme. Of course, despite its 'quasi-governmental' nature, UNRWA has no legal authority to exercise the very important "international protection" function exercised by the UNHCR on behalf of other refugee populations.

### The Role of the United Nations High Commissioner for Refugees

When the United Nations replaced the League of Nations in 1945, it recognized from the outset that the task of caring for refugees was a matter of international concern and that , in keeping with its charter, the community of States should assume collective responsibility for those fleeing persecution.

The task of caring for refugees-indicates an international concern because of two basic reasons. First, there exists a clear humanitarian aspect of the matter duly recognized by the Charter of the United Nations which has distinct provisions for respect and protection of human rights. The second reason is' the basic fact that it inevitably involves the interests of more than one State. The another reason was indeed fundamental based on sheer necessity arising out of the need for effective tackling of the problem of refugees. It could not be dealt with by mere negotiation or mediation or intervention or other methods known for resolution of international problems and disputes. The special aspects of the problem needed a proper organisation with regular manpower running it to create some impression towards resolving the grave problem of multitude of human beings totally displaced and rendered helpless without a home and often without food and necessary means of living. The solution dictated the establishment of a regular organisation as a sheer necessity and this does furnish the raison d'etre of the numerous refugee organizations that came into being before 1946 and also after the UN came into existence like the IRO and subsequently the U.N. High Commissioner for Refugees.

Here it is interesting to note that when the General Assembly of the United Nations decided on 3rd December 1949 to establish an agency to succeed IRO, governmental opinion was no more unanimous than it had been four years earlier. However, the countries, in favour of the new body were generally agreed that its main function should be international protection. Countries outside Europe believed that the problem of refugees and displaced persons resulting from the second world war was largely solved, mainly through their departure for overseas lands. These countries thought that a small organization with limited functions and a short life-span of, for example, three years was all that was needed to deal with the residual group of non-integrated refugees then within IRO's mandate. Accordingly, the IRCI was replaced by the Office of the *United Nations High Commissioner for Refugees (UNHCR)* on 1st January 1951 and it was to be for a period of 3 years in the first instance evide General Assembly Resolution 319(iv) of December 3,1949 and 428 (v) of 14th December 1950. The Statute of UNHCR, adopted by a General Assembly resolution in December 1950,11 outlines the responsibility of the Office, the most important of which are-

> "providing international protection.... and .... seeking permanent solutions for the problems of refugees."

The Statute placed UNHCR under the authority of the UN General Assembly. It is a subsidiary body, following directives received from the Assembly or from the Economic and Social Council (ECOSOC). According to the very first Article of the Statute, the High Commissioner acts "under the authority of the UN General Assembly" and Art. 3 prescribes that he shall follow "policy directives given him by the General Assembly or the Economic and Social, Council." In 1951, the ECOSOC at its 13th Session established the Advisory Committee on Refugees to guide the High Commissioner, at his request, in the exercise of his functions. In the beginning of 1955 the General Assembly by its Resolution 832 (viii) and ECOSOC by 565 (xix) adopted in October 1954 and March 1955 respectively, reconstituted the Advisory Committee as an Executive Committee known as UNREF Committee which retained the advisory function of its predecessor. However, again it was in 1959 that the UNREF Committee was replaced by the *Executive Committee of the High Commissioner's Programme.* The Executive Committee reviews the use of the Emergency Fund, and the administration of Special Trust Funds, and advises the High Commissioner, at his request, in the exercise of his function under the statute of his office. It is assisted in the execution of its functions by the Subcommittee of the whole on International Protection and the Subcommittee on Administrative and Financial Matter. At present the Executive Committee consists of 50 member-states and India is one of its members. Member either of the United Nations or one of its specialised agencies, to be elected by ECOSOC on the widest possible geographical basis from those States with a demonstrated interest in, and devotion to the solution of the refugee problem. UNHCR activities within the framework of Special Programme were reported to the Executive Committee from its inception.

The general control of the U.N. over the Office of the High Commissioner is exercised by various methods such as the annual report on the later's activities which has to be submitted through the ECOSOC and is first considered by the Third Committee of the U.N. General-Assembly. Again the administrative and financial aspect of the activities of UNHCR are considered by the Advisory Committee on Administrative and Budgetary Questions (ACABQ) as well as the Fifth Committee of the General Assembly. Thus not only the policy directives but also the finances of the High Commissioner are in the hands of the Fifth and Third Committee of the U.N. as well as the ECOSOC. The High Commissioner for Refugees is elected by the United Nations General Assembly on the nomination of the Secretary General. The present High Commissioner, Mrs. Sadako Ogata (Japan), took up the office on January 1,1991.

**The Subjects of UNHCR-jurisdiction and "Persons of Concern"**

There are at least four types of persons that form the legitimate subjects of UNHCR. These are : the so-called statutory", "convention", "Protocol" and "mandate" refugees The first type-statutory refugee-is severely restricted by limitations of time and geography. The second type-convention refugee-as it appears in the Convention (and the Statute) is also greatly restricted by qualifications of time and geography. But, as these qualifications are removed by the Protocol, the potential membership of the class of the third type-protocol refugee is global and without limit as to time. The fourth type mandate refugee-referring to the "mandate" of the High Commissioner, is similarly broad.

The competence of the High Commissioner extends in varying degrees to all four types of refugees. These are not mutually exclusive, it is quite possible for an individual to be classified under more than one type. But, only the latter two types (Protocol and mandate) are relevant to the more recent refugee situations. Here it may further be noted that the statutory refugees are those refugees defined in paragraph 6A(i) of the Statute, which is identical in scope to Art IA(i) of the 1951 Convention. The Protocol also applies to stâtutory refugees. This type of refugee includes a number of clearly defined categories of refugee which arose in relation to various peoples of Europe and Asia before, during and shortly after World War II.

A Convention refugee is basically any person who "as a result of events occurring before January 1,1951 and owing to well-founded fear of being persecuted .... is outside the country of his nationality and is unable or, owing to such fear, is unwilling to avail himself of the protection of that country *(Art., IA(2) of the 1951 Convention).* This formulation coincides almost exactly with paragraph *6A(ii) of the Statute,* which includes such persons within the High Commissioner's competence. But, the Convention's definition is broader, as it contains an additional ground for fear of persecution. The Statute refers to "race, religion, nationality or political opinion"; the Convention refers to these grounds as well as to "membership of a particular social group". The protocol applies the same grounds as the Convention except in respect of two fundamental differences. The forementioned limitations of time (i.e. the 1951 dateline) and geography do not apply to protocol refugees.

However, it was General, Assembly resolution of 20th November, 1959, which drew a clear distinction for the first time between refugees within the mandate and refugees who do not come within the competence of the United Nations, in respect of whom the High Commissioner was authorised to use his good offices in the transgressors of contribution designed to assist them. So, until 1964 some, refugees were described as benefitting from the High Commissioner's good -offices, and others as falling within his mandate. From 1966, however, the General Assembly ceased to make this distinction, requesting the High Commissioner to "continue to provide international protection to refugees who are his concern, within the limits of his competence, and to promote permanent solutions to their problems". Later, in December, 1972, to allow UNHCR to assist in the repatriation of Sudanese refuges, from neighbouring countries and also to resettle those who had' been displaced within their own country, the Assembly referred at one and the same time to refugees and displaced persons as coming within the competence of the High Commissioner. In 1975 an important step was taken when Resolution 3454 (XXX) of 9 December reaffirmed in its preamble "the essentially humanitarian character of the activities of the High Commissioner for the benefit of refugees and displaces persons".

**Assistance Activities of the United Nations High Commissioner for Refugees**

In any refugee relief situation, one agency should be designated as the primary operating agency, with responsibility for coordinating relief activities and ensuring that all refugees received the basic, minimal level of assistance. The three primary tasks that must be carried out by any coordinator of relief operations include the responsibility to ensure

(1) that all refugees have equal access to the services being offered;

(2) that all refugees receive a basic, minimal standard of care and support while in refugee camps; and

(3) the coordination of the services offered by various operational partners (usually international voluntary agencies), so as to guarantee that no gaps in services or levels of service occur:

In the heat of a refugee emergency, the immediate priority is to save lives. Two factors, in particular, are crucial: One is to protect the displaced people from being forced back into the areas from which they have fled, and the other is to supply them with food, water, health care, shelter and sanitation. Meeting the physical needs of people in emergency is the more tangible response of the two, and often seems to dominate the agenda of emergency assistance. But protection should be built into emergency management from the very beginning. The challenge is to provide aid in a way that shields people from further persecution and violence, while simultaneously laying the foundations for lasting solutions to their predicament. It is absolutely true that the speed and efficiency of the initial response to a refugee emergency affect the welfare and in some cases the very survival of the people concerned; they may also influence the prospects for solutions. The office of the United Nations High Commissioner for Refugees (UNHCR) is viewed increasingly as the humanitarian arm of the United Nations. The agency's work is being transformed in the post-cold war era by its efforts to respond to the proliferation of conflicts and cause of displacement that have produced nearly 20 million refugees and another 24 million,, internally displaced persons. Prom the mountains of northern Iraq to the besieged city of Sarajevo UNHCR has been required to respond in new ways to new responsibilities.

UNHCR has a major role in co-ordinating aid to refugees, Except in special circumstances, its material assistance - activities are conducted through national or local authorities of the country concerned, other organizations of the United Nations system, non-governmental organizations, to private technical agencies.

In this context it may be submitted that no explicit enabling provisions for UNHCR's' material assistance functions can be found in Paragraph 8 of the Statute which sets out the High Commissioner's responsibilities in greater detail, or in the 1951 Convention; neither has the question of humanitarian assistance been covered by subsequent conventions dealing with refugees.

**The Financing of the Office**

In accordance with paragraph 10 of the Statute of 1950 the High Commissioner administers funds both public and private which he received as earmarked for refugees.

(i) *Public Source* - Under this head would come

(a) the limited subsidy received from the regular budget of the UN which is earmarked for being exclusively used for administrative costs of the Office of the High Commissioner as well as;

(b) Contributions made by Governments in response to the appeal made by the High Commissioner in accordance with the directive received from the General Assembly of the UN.

(ii) *Private Source*-Again, Private funds which represent voluntary contributions from :

(a) non-governmental organisations, and

(b) private individuals, constitute another important source for financing the activities of the Organisation, which centre around assistance to refugees in one form or another. Here, it may be added that the High Commissioner is authorised to make appeals for funds needed to provide material assistance for refugees under terms of the General Assembly Resolution 1166 (111) which lays down the modalities for the review by the Executive Committee of UNHCR's annual material assistance programmes. UNHCR's assistance activities divide broadly into General and Special, programmes. The former comprise activities financed through the annual budget, while special Programmes comprise activities financed., from funds constituted for particular purposes and with particular conditions, and may be for the benefit of a wide range of needy persons. These programmes, seek wherever possible to foster lasting solutions, pending the realisation of

> which care and maintenance will be provided while encouraging self-reliance when feasible.

Here it is worthwhile to mention that the General Programmes adopted so far able the High Commissioner to deal with new refugee situations between sessions of the Executive Committee by drawing on the Emergency Fund to finance immediate survival needs, making adjustments in allocations, modifying Project allocations, drawing on savings made on other allocations. In the event, however, of large-scale material assistance-Project being required immediately for assistance to a new group of refugees', the High Commissioner would consult the Executive Committee.

**Material Assistance -General Developments Since the Inception of UNHCR**

The General Assembly, in its resolution 538(VI) B, adopted at its Sixth Session in February, 1952, authorised the High Commissioner to issue an appeal for funds, under paragraph 10 of the Statute, to enable UNHCR to give emergency aid to the most needy groups of refugees. The fund that was thus constituted referred to as the United Nations Refugee Emergency Fund, remained in operation until the establishment , of the UNREF Programme in 1954. Soon after the creation of UNHCR, an Advisory Committee had been set up to assist the High Commissioner. In 1955 the Advisory Committee was replaced by the UNREF Executive Committee which in turn was replaced by the Executive Committee of the Programme of UNHCR. The Executive Committee, appointed by the Economic and Social Council and now comprising of 50 members, remains the guiding body of the office.

In 1958 the General Assembly passed a resolution 1166(XII) in relation to the assistance Programmes of the UNHCR.

Under the terms of this resolution and of decisions subsequently taken by the UNREF Executive Committee, the High Commissioner was authorised to put into effect an annual assistance Programme-nowadays referred to as General Programmes. The Projects and financial targets submitted under these programmes are subject to prior approval by the Executive Committee. The High Commissioner was also authorised to establish an emergency fund. He furthermore, required to submit an annual progress report on the implementation of his programme.

As and when new large-scale problems concerning refugees arose, UNHCR was called to provide essential material assistance under Special Programmes in keeping with specific resolutions adopted by the General Assembly and ECOSOC to that effect. Furthermore, pursuant to Resolution 2956 (XXVII), adopted by the General Assembly in December, 1972, the High Commissioner was requested, at the invitation of the Secretary General, to continue to participate in those humanitarian endeavours of the United Nations for which his office has particular expertise and experience. "The structural change paved the way for deeper and more comprehensive extensions of UNHCR's competence for material assistance functions. A dual approach in the progressive widening of UNHCR's mandate, in the form of greater capacity for humanitarian assistance and expanded categories of persons eligible for protection, emerged from the fundamental responsibility to seek solutions to the refugee problem".

A wide recognition of UNHCR's non-mandate responsibility occurred when the High Commissioner was requested in 1961 by General Assembly Resolution 1625 (XVI) to continue to "pursue his activities on behalf of the refugees within the mandate, or those for whom he extends his good offices". The effect of these provisions was to authorise the High Commissioner to use his good offices on behalf of any person considered to be a refugee who was not a mandate refugee or within the competence of any other UN organ. The achievement of the good offices resolutions was thus described by a former High Commissioner essentially as enabling large scale operations to be conducted, centred entirely on the provision of material assistance. However, in the year 1965, the General Assembly passed a Resolution 2039 (XX) and abandoned the distinction between refugees within the mandate and refugees covered by the High Commissioner's good offices.

Throughout the 1960's and 1970's growing refugee problems relating to an increasingly wide range of uprooted people highlighted the need for a corresponding increase and change in field activities. In 1975, the General Assembly passed a Resolution 3454(XXX), in which the preamble specifically reaffirmed 'the eminently humanitarian character of the activities of the High Commissioner for the benefit of refugees and displaced persons'.

**Main Aspects of UNHCR Material Assistance Activities**

UNHCR material assistance activities include emergency relief, assistance in voluntary repatriation or local integration, resettlement through migration to other countries, as well as counselling, education, and legal assistance.

(i) *Emergency Relief* is provided mainly in the form of care and maintenance of new refugees or displaced persons when a variety of basic essentials such as food, shelter and medical aid are required on a large scale at short notice. In recent years, this type of aid has been needed in Africa, Asia, and Central America, just to ensure survival.

(ii) *Assistance in Voluntary Repatriation* - In such cases, the assistance element consists of helping refugees, wherever possible, to overcome practical difficulties concerning their voluntary repatriation. It also allows UNHCR to ensure that the refugees are given basic help upon arrival in their homestead.

(iii) *Local Integration* -The object of local integration is to assist refugees and displaced persons to become self-supporting in their country of residence and or of first asylum. This is done in a number of ways, such as by providing refugees with loans or grants to establish themselves in a profession, assisting them through vocational training to learn a skill etc.

(iv) *Resettlement through migration* - From its inception, UNHCR has been actively engaged in the promotion of resettlement through migration, in close co-operation with interested governments and voluntary agencies concerned with the resettlement of refugees.

(v) *Education* has proved to be particularly important in facilitating the integration of refugees. Educational assistance of primary and secondary level is made available under UNHCR General Programmes.

(vi) *Counselling,* which is provided under various UNHCR Programmes, is particularly important in helping refuges to opt for an appropriate solution to their problems and to avail themselves of such facilities as may be open to them.

(vii) The *rehabilitation* of disabled refugees is mostly undertaken in close co-operation with voluntary agencies which implement special local programmes of assistance and treatment. A further response to the needs of disabled refugees is UNHCR's Promotion of Special Resettlement schemes known as the "Tenor - More Plan". Under -this plan, several resettlement countries admit ten or more handicapped refugees and their families per year.

(viii) *Legal assistance* is provided to help individual refugees with administrative formalities in their country of residence. It is also provided to refugees who are involved in court cases affecting their refugee status. It may be summarised that though material assistance activities of the High Commissioner stated modestly it has now assumed an increased proportion.

**Co-operation with Other Bodies**

Para 8 of the Statute of the UNHCR provides for cooperation with all members of the international community. With the increase and diversification of UNHCR's activities, relation with member agencies of the United Nations System, as well as with inter-governmental and non-governmental organizations (NGOs), have continued to strengthen. UNHCR draws on the expertise of other organizations of the United Nations system experienced in matters such as food production (FAC), health measures (WHO), education (UNESCO), child welfare (UNICEF) and vocational training (ILO).

The participation of the World Food Programme (WFP) is particularly important in supplying food until such time as the refugees are able to grow their own crops or become self-sufficient through other activities. Close contact is also maintained with the Resident Co-ordinantors /Representatives of the United Nations/United Nations Development Programme (UNDP). In areas where UNHCR is not represented, UNDP representatives frequently administer UNHCR-financed projects and act on UNHCR's behalf in relations with Governments. The World Bank and UNHCR have co-operated in planning, financing and implementing projects aimed at promoting self-reliance through, for example, agricultural activities and at creating employment opportunities for refugees in their country of asylum.

In addition to these and other members of the United Nations system co-operating with UNHCR in their respective fields, inter-governmental organizations play an important part in UNHCR's activities. The European Community (EEC) is instrumental in providing contributions, both in cash and kind, and in the implementation of legal instruments. The EEC also extends considerable moral and political support in the search for solutions to refugee problems. The International Organization for Migration (IOM) organizes the transportation of refugee migrants. There is also a long-standing tradition of co-operating between UNHCR, the International Committee of the Red Cross (ICRC) and the League of Red Cross Societies (LRCS).

UNHCR co-ordinates activities with the' Organization of African Unity (OAU) within the framework of the Joint Working Group established to monitor progress in the implementation of recommendations adopted at the Conference on the Situation of African Refugees held in Arusha in 1979. The International Conference on Assistance to refugees in Africa (ICARA), held in Geneva in April 1981, was sponsored jointly by the Secretary-General of the United Nations, the OAU and UNHCR, The second International Conference on Assistance to Refugees in Africa (ICARA II) took place in Geneva in July 1984 Under the same auspices except that UNDP also participated in the Steering Committee in recognition of the development aspect of many of the projects submitted to the Conference. The latest of the Conferences organized under these co-operative arrangements, the International Conference on the Plight of Refugees, Returnees and Displaced Persons in Southern Africa (SARRED) was held in Oslo, Norway in August 1988. Relations with the

Organization of America States (OAS) have continued, with special emphasis at the moment on UNHCR's programme for Central American refugees. One of the most important areas of co-operation with the OAS in 1988 and 1989 concerned preparations for the International Conference on Central American Refugees (CIREFCA) which was held in Guatemala City in May 1989. Several discussions were held with the OAS in preparation for that Conference.

Within the United Nations, UNHCR provided organizational and other preparatory support for the International Conference on Indo-Chinese Refugees (ICIR) which was convened by the Secretary-General and took place in Geneva in June 1989 to consider a new approach to the problems of Indo-Chinese refugees and asylum-seekers. Close co-operation with the League of Arab States continues, while an Agreement was signed in July 1988 between the Organization of the Islamic Conference and UNHCR, thus consolidating co-operation in areas of mutual interest. A number of countries have governmental or semi-official organizations dealing with refugees. However, over the decades, perhaps the most sustained and devoted service to the cause of refugees has been provided by voluntary agencies. Voluntary agencies or non-governmental organizations frequently act as UNHCR operational partners in the implementation of specific projects.

They also play an important part in the migration and resettlement of refugees. Other voluntary agencies are of great importance by virtue of the funds they make available for refugee assistance. UNHCR has direct contact with some 200 NGOs, the majority of which are helping in operational or other ways to assist refugees. UNHCR also maintains close contact with the International Council of Voluntary Agencies (ICVA) in Geneva.

**Some Recent Aspects**

The number of people of concern to UNHCR has increased in recent years: 17 million in 1991, 23 million in 1993 and more than 27 million at the beginning of 1995. Of this, nearly 14.5 million are refugees-people who have crossed on international border and been granted asylum in another state.

Close to 40 per cent of all refugees were in Africa, and slightly over 30 per cent in Asia. Almost 60 per cent of the internally-displaced persons assisted by UNHCR were in the former Yugoslavia and 30 per cent in the former Soviet Union. The largest populations of concern to UNHCR were in Bosnia and Herzegovina (2-7 million displaced persons and victims of war), the Islamic Republic of Iran (2.5 million Afghan and Iraqe refugees) and Pakistan (1.5 million, mainly Afghan refugees). Since the start of the 1990s, the UNHCR has mounted emergency operations in an accelerating series of crises.

These have included the flight of 1.8 million Iraqi Kurds to the Islamic Republic of Iran and the' border between Turkey and Iraq; the war that has produced nearly 4 million 'refugees, displaced people and other ' victims in former Yugoslavia; the arrival of about 330,000- refugees in Kenya, the majority from Somalia an exodus of around .260,000 refugees from Myanmar into Bangladesh; and the influx of some 250,000 refugees-from Togo into Benin and Ghana. In addition, crises in the Transcaucasus and Central Asia led UNHCR to dispatch Emergency Response Teams to cope with some 1.5 million displaced persons in Armenia, Azerbaijan and Tajikistan in December 1992. At the end of 1993. UNHCR began to deal with a refugee crisis in Burundi; in April 1994, this emergency was compounded by a fresh exodus of refugees from Rwanda, which put the number of refugees and returnees in the region in need of assistance at over 8,00,000.

A $ 25 million emergency fund allows UNHCR to provide a rapid response to new refugee situations. If this initial assistance proves insufficient to meet the full range of needs arising from a large-scale movement of refugees, special appeals are launched to raise funds from the international community.

In order to be able to respond effectively to emergencies, UNHCR has established a structure of emergency response teams and made arrangements to pre-position and stockpile relief supplies. To provide yet further flexibility, stand-by arrangement have been made with the Danish and Norwegian Refugee Councils and the United Nations Volunteers (UNV) for the quick development of staff to emergency operations in any part of the world.

In 1992, UNHCR continued to implement the High Commissioner's three-pronged strategy of Prevention, Preparedness and solutions. UNHCR began to provide assistance hot only to refugees, returnees and displaced persons addressing the needs of entire communitie's rather than focussing on individuals but also, in the case of the former Yugoslavia, to people under a direct threat of expulsion or threatened by the form of persecution now known as "ethnic cleansing". More than 600 UNHCR staff in the former Yugoslavia helped not only to distribute relief to the displaced and besiezed populations, but also to meet their protection needs. In Somalia, UNHCR established presence across the border from Kenya, and brought in food and assistance in an effort to stabilize population movements and eventually create conditions to the return of refugees. In South-eastern Ethiopia, UNHCR joined efforts with other United Nations organizations to address the needs of entire communities with the goal of stabilizing the population. UNHCR's *Open Relief Centres* (*ORC*) in Sri Lanka have become heavens of safety, accepted and respected by both warring parties. In terms of preparedness, the office continued to strengthen its emergency preparedness and response capacity, recognizing that the capacity to deliver is a necessary prerequisite for improved system-wide co-ordination to address complex humanitarian emergencies.

In 1993, UNHCR has mounted emergency programmes for over three million people in the former Yugoslavia, for some 420,000 refugees in Kenya, for some 260,000 refugees from Myanmar in Bangladesh and for the continued influx of asylum-seekers from Bhutan into Nepal. Emergency Response Teams were sent to Armenia, Azerbaijan and Tajikistan in early December, 1992, making the area a new focus of UNHCR concern and activity. In early 1993, in Africa the office began to cope with a new influx of some 200,000 refugees from Togo into Benin and Ghana.

As to solutions, during the same period, UNHCR helped some 24 million refugees to return home voluntarily-including over 1.2 million to Afghanistan, some 360,000 to Cambodia and tens of thousands to Ethopia; Progress continued in the local integration and repatriation of thousands of Central Americans through the process initiated in the framework of the International Conference on Central American Refugees (CIREFCA).

With the encouragement of the Executive Committee and the United Nations General Assembly in its resolution 47/105(192), UNHCR has sought to strengthen its cooperation with the human rights bodies of the United Nations with a view to promoting effective responses to human rights problems which are generating or threaten to generate, flow of refugees and displaced persons, or which impede voluntary return.

Here it may be mentioned that in 1992 the total expenditure of UNHCR under General programmes (including Emergency Fund) amounted to $ 382.1 million. With regard to Special Programmes (which include programmes funded through appeals by the United 'Nations Secretary General) expenditure related to 1992 reached $ .689.8 million. Thus, total voluntary funds expenditure related to 1992 activities amounted to $ 1,701.9 million. In addition, the Regular Budget contribution to UNHCR amounted to $ 21.2 million. In terms of volume of activities and related expenditure, 1992 therefore represented a record, year in UNHCR's history, exceeding 1991 expenditure by some 24 per cent. It also reflected an unprecedented effort by the donor community in support of humanitarian initiatives world wide. The 1993 General Programmes target, as approved by the Executive Committee at its meeting on December 17,1992, stands at $ 413.6 million. Projections for 1993 under Special Programmes amount to $ 959.7 million.

# 8

# Cessation of Refugee Status

> "Ambition, as you know, can cut two ways: It was ambition and its fueling force, perseverance, which gave us the electric light, the telephone, and all the other servants of our mechanized state. On the other hand, it was ambition which produced Mussolini and Hitler and Khrushchev, without dipping deeper into history for hor-rendous examples. May we not conclude, therefore, that ambition needs some sort of checkrein to keep it from getting out of hand."
>
> —*T. Harry Thompson*

Issues of cessation of and exclusion from refugee status may arise in two contexts. First, since the incorporation into Canadian law in 1989 of Articles 1 (C), (E) and (F) of the Convention, the Immigration and Refugee Board may determine that a person who otherwise meets the refugee definition is, as of the date of the hearing of the claim, within the scope of a cessation or exclusion clause. Such a person is not a Convention refugee and is subject to removal. Alternatively, a cessation hearing may be convened before the Board subsequent to the recognition of refugee status. If the case for cessation is made out at this level, the refugee not already landed as a permanent resident is subject to removal. If landing has already taken place, the individual ought not to continue to benefit from Convention based rights, such as protection against *refoulement,* but should nonetheless be subject to the ordinary rules which govern loss of permanent resident status.

This chapter considers the scope of the Convention's cessation and exclusion clauses, with a view to identifying the limited situations in which even persons who are or have been genuinely at risk of serious harm grounded in civil or political status may not qualify as refugees. Because these clauses are to be applied only in relation to persons who otherwise present a *prima facie* need for protection, they ought reasonably to be strictly construed. Nonetheless, it is clear that a state's duty under international refugee law extends neither to persons who benefit from sufficient protection elsewhere, nor to those whose own actions are inconsistent with the basic human rights undertaking.

The discussion here is divided into three parts. First, when can it be said that a refugee has regained the protection of her state of origin, such that she no longer requires refugee status? Second and alternatively, under what circumstances, is surrogate national or international protection sufficient to meet the refugee's needs? Finally, which categories of persons are genuinely unworthy of international protection as refugees?

### Persons Who Have Regained the Protection of Their State of Origin

It is a truism that the happiest solution to involuntary migration is the resumption of protection within a refugee's state of origin, such that she can return home in safety. Under the Convention, the sufficiency of national protection may be manifested in either of two ways. First, the refugee herself may elect to entrust her safety to the state of origin by way of re-availment of its formal protection, re-acquisition of its nationality, or re-establishment in its territory. Behaviour of this sort is deemed inconsistent with the refugee's professed need for protection, and gives rise to an objectively rebuttable presumption of cessation of status. Second, the authorities in the country of reception may determine that human rights conditions in the country of origin have improved to such an extent that-the once-present genuine risk of persecution is no longer a reality, thus opening the way for the refugee's return.

**Voluntary Re-availment of National Protection**

Cessation based on re-availment of national protection generally involves the consideration of efforts by a refugee to secure diplomatic or consular protection from the authorities of the state of which she is formally a citizen. Typically, the refugee will seek the issuance or renewal of a passport or other identity document, although a minority of cases centres on more formal requests for intervention or representation of the claimant's interests. Because actions of this sort are technically viewed as implying protection, it is arguable that the refugee exhibits a willingness to entrust her welfare to the state of origin, and hence no longer requires protection under international law.

Such an interpretation of this cessation clause represents a formal view of the notion of protection. As Atle Grahl-Madsen points out, "... a person may seldom have well-founded fear of being persecuted by the members of the foreign service of his home country; the pertinent fact is therefore that he fears persecution in the case of his return to his country of origin". It is V simply a legal fiction to assume that more than an exceedingly small percentage of persons who avail themselves of a state's consular facilities do so as a demonstration of either political loyalty or trust.

Rather, the practical exigencies of life - travel, enrolment in school, professional accreditation, etc. - may simply require a person genuinely at risk of persecution to contact the external office of her state of origin to secure essential documentation. Too, many persons renew identity documents as a matter of routine, with no thought to the legal ramifications of their act. The disparity between the legal formalism familiar to the drafters of the Convention and the common understandings of most people has required the strict construction of this clause in order to avoid undercutting the protective mandate of refugee law.

First, the request for formal protection must be made voluntarily. As noted by the French delegate who introduced the clause, "... a person lost his status of refugee only if he expressly wished to do so and, for that purpose, performed a number of voluntary acts ...... The request is not voluntary if, as in the case of *Wilfredo Alejandro Zubieta,* the refugee is seeking only to comply with an administrative directive issued by the country of reception, or indeed is under the mistaken impression that the maintenance of a valid passport or other status is expected of him.

Second, the diplomatic request must be made as an act of re-availment of protection, thus implying an intention to have one's interests defended by the issuing state. In contrast, most ordinary, purely practical forms of diplomatic contact, such as requests for the certification of educational or occupational qualifications, or access to personal birth, marital, and other records, are dictated by practical necessity, rather than by a desire for protection. Canadian decisions have usually acknowledged this principle, even if sometimes failing to apply it. A case in point is *Carlos Antonio Munoz Munizaga,* in which Chairman Scott explicitly juxtaposed principle and practice:

> Adopting the view of the [French] Commission des Recours that the motive for obtaining a passport must be examined -an eminently sensible approach since it relates directly to the aspect of "well-founded fear" which is an essential part of the definition of refugee - we ask, why did Munoz obtain a Chilean passport in Vancouver? To go to Sweden. In the circumstances of this case, he was benefitting from his national status by applying for, obtaining, and using, a document entitling him to the protection of his own country in his travels abroad. He has therefore lost any refugee status he may have had.

Yet the reason Munoz sought the passport was because he had been advised that his chances of securing asylum were better in Sweden than in Canada, inconsequence of which he initially elected to travel onward - surely a motive which is the antithesis of a desire to secure Chile's protection! A similarly inappropriate application of the notion of re-availment is found in the decision of *Tarek Mohamed Shafey Wahba,* involving an Egyptian claimant who reported the loss of his Egyptian passport to that country's embassy in Ottawa. Even though he did not apply for a replacement passport and secured a World Services Authority passport for his travel needs, the Board viewed the simple act of - reporting the loss of the passport as indicating "that he was not unwilling to avail himself of the protection of his country". These decisions fail to come to grips with the *real* reasons which cause refugees to contact the diplomatic authorities of their country of origin. In particular, decision-makers have often relied on an inaccurate assumption that receipt of travel documentation is inherently a means of securing national protection:

> ... it seems high time to dispel an idea that is all too prevalent - and, what is more, false - of exactly what

> a passport is. A passport is no more, in fact and in law, than a travel document issued by a country's proper authorities to allow one of its nationals to travel abroad and, if necessary, to call upon the services of its consular authorities in the foreign countries visited to provide the holder of the document with proper protection. The fact of holding a passport, even if it is valid and issued legally, in no way constitutes a guarantee that protection will be provided ....

This position was acknowledged during the Convention's drafting, and is generally recognized in public international law:

> ... there is no duty on the part of a State to exercise protection over its citizens abroad; whether or not to exercise protection remains in the absolute discretion of the state.... The municipal law of the issuing state may provide that the issuance of a passport to one of its nationals will be a guarantee that the state will protect the bearer while abroad. Nevertheless, the state can breach that guarantee without violating international law.

Since there is no automatic linkage between the issuance or renewal of a passport and the granting of protection, it is critical that the real reason it is being sought form part of the determination authority's considerations. Unless the refugee's motive is genuinely the entrusting of her interests to the protection of the state of her nationality, the requisite intent is absent.

Third, the clause does not apply unless diplomatic or consular protection is actually given. As originally introduced by the French delegate, the clause provided that any person who attempted to secure diplomatic or consular protection from her state of origin would lose her refugee status, whether or not protection was actually granted. This strict approach was forcefully rejected by the British, American, and Peruvian delegates, leading to intervention by the Chairman in favour of an interpretation which would limit cessation to circumstances in which formal protection was in fact forthcoming:

> ... the opening words. . . namely "This Convention shall not apply to any refugee enjoying the protection of a government", made it clear that whatever claims he had made, such claims had been successful, otherwise he would not be enjoying the protection of a government.

An American amendment substituting the final language, "has voluntarily re-availed himself of, in place of the original French version, "he voluntarily claims anew", was then adopted to give effect to the Chairman's ruling that the receipt of protection is key.

The requisite elements of voluntarism, specific intent, and consummation constrain the frequency with which cessation based on voluntary re-availment of protection is likely to occur. This cautious confining of the clause's application is, however, appropriate in view of the risk that a purely formal or practical contact with foreign diplomatic personnel might otherwise put a refugee at risk of return to persecution.

**Voluntary Re-acquisition of Nationality**

While the legal import of availing oneself of diplomatic or consular services maybe ambiguous, the decision to secure anew the citizenship of the state in which persecution was feared raises more poignantly the refugee's continuing need for protection. Because nationality is widely understood to imply a bond of allegiance between state and citizen, the refugee who resumes the citizenship of her state of origin must rebut the presumption that she may return to that country in safety. Specific intent, therefore, is hot requisite to cessation under this clause, although the requirements of voluntarism and consummation discussed in the preceding part apply here as well:

> Like the provision of Article 1(c)(I), the provision presently considered has its principal *raison detre* as a means to bring about, the termination of refugee 'status for those who wilfully or for no good reason take a positive step in order to normalize their relations with the authorities of their country of origin or in order to reap the benefits due to nationals of that country under international law or comity. Article I (C)(2) should be applied very reluctantly indeed to other categories of refugees, the continued existence of well-founded fear of persecution being the overriding consideration in cases of doubt.

Thus, for example, re-acquisition of nationality through operation of law upon marriage or otherwise may fail to meet the requirement of voluntarism, and hence not suffice to deprive a refugee of her status. Nor is it enough to show that the refugee could have re-acquired her former citizenship but failed to do so, since there is no consummation of the act of protection. The overriding concern is whether there is an act of re-acquisition of citizenship which is truly indicative of a normalization of relations between the refugee and her state of origin.

The scope of this cessation clause is also textually limited to a narrow subset of refugees. Persons who have continued to be formal citizens of their state of origin during their time as refugees are obviously not in a position to *acquire* the nationality of that country. Too, because it speaks to reacquisition of nationality, this cessation clause does not apply to persons who are stateless from birth, but only to those who have at some point been denationalized or who have successfully renounced their citizenship, and who then go on to have their status as citizens reinstated.

**Voluntary Re-establishment in the Country in Which Persecution was Feared**

Re-establishment in the state of origin is perhaps the clearest indication that a refugee no longer views herself as being at risk. In voluntarily taking up residence in the country which induced her flight, the refugee is in the most direct way possible signalling her willingness to entrust her welfare to that state.

The Convention requires freely chosen re-establishment, not mere return, before cessation ensues. The original draft of this clause, which would have revoked the refugee status of any person who "returns to his country of former nationality", was rejected by the *Ad Hoc* Committee on the ground that it might bar persons who had been forcibly repatriated to their state of origin, as well as those who had chosen to return to their country of origin only temporarily. The substitute language which sets the cessation threshold at voluntary re-establishment in the country in which persecution was feared" was thus intended to ensure that only persons who have willingly resettled in their state of origin are subject to cessation of refugee status. As Paul Weis notes,

> If a person returns to his country of origin for a temporary stay without re- establishing himself, and then returns to the country where he was recognized as a refugee, this should not, lead to *ipso facto* loss of refugee status.

Re-establishment requires more than mere physical

presence, and a greater commitment to the country of origin than is evinced, for example, by a temporary return to visit an ailing parent or to bring out relatives, friends, or property. Careful scrutiny of more prolonged and frequent visits for such purposes as holidays or business is warranted, however, since at some point the degree of attachment may qualify as re-establishment. While an occasional visit of up to a few weeks is too transitory to sustain the cessation of status, a regular presence in the state of origin for a significant part of the year is *prime facie* inconsistent with a continued need for protection. The claimant should, bear the onus in such circumstances to demonstrate that she is objectively unable to benefit from protection of basic human rights in her country of origin, and thus continues to be & refugee.

It is not appropriate, however, to construe this cessation clause effectively to penalize refugees who return to "test the waters" in their state of origin. If refugees are to be encouraged to attempt voluntary repatriation, generally viewed as the most desirable solution to refugeehood, they must have some assurance that they can resume refugee status in the event that actual conditions at home prove unsafe. Before a finding of cessation based on voluntary re-establishment is made, therefore, both the facts underlying the original, successful claim to refugee status and post re-establishment factors should be taken into account. If the totality of the evidence demonstrates a forward-looking, genuine risk of persecution, this cessation clause is not a bar to continued recognition as a refugee.

**Change of Circumstances**

Unlike the forms of cessation discussed thus far which are initiated by the voluntary act of a refugee, cessation due to change of circumstances is the prerogative of an asylum state which is satisfied that protection is once more viable in the refugee's state of origin. The clause was intended to allow a state to divest itself of the protection "burden" when the government of the home country is judged to have become an appropriate guardian of the rights of its involuntary expatriates:

> To take the case of the aged belonging to the "hard core" of refugees, it could hardly be agreed that the government of a country which had returned to democratic ways should fail to take over the burden of that category of refugees.... [France] was quite prepared to continue to assist such refugees so long as such assistance was necessary. But if their country reverted to a democratic regime, the obligation to assist them should not fall perforce upon the French Government. . . . France had merely said that she did not wish to be under an obligation to continue to provide assistance to refugees who could seek the protection of their country of origin.

The drafters' focus- on reversion to democracy highlights the magnitude of change which should exist-before the consideration of cessation is warranted. First, the change must be of substantial political significance, in the sense that, the power structure under which persecution was deemed a real possibility no longer exists. The collapse of the persecutory regime, coupled with the holding of genuinely free and democratic elections, the assumption of power by a government committed to human rights, and a guarantee of fair treatment for enemies of the predecessor regime by way of amnesty or otherwise is the appropriate indicator of a meaningful change of circumstances. It would, in contrast, be premature to consider cessation simply because relative calm has been restored in a country still governed by an oppressive political structure. Similarly, the mere fact that a democratic and safe local or regional government has been established is V insufficient insofar as the national government still poses a risk to the refugee. Second, there must be reason to believe that the substantial political change is truly effective. Because, as noted in a dissenting opinion in Ruiz Angel Jesus Gonzales, ". . . there is often a long distance between the pledging and the doing. . .", it ought not to be assumed that formal change will necessarily be immediately effective:

> . . . there were free elections [in Uruguay] on March 1, 1985 that put an end to 12 years of military government. According to [the U.S. Country Reports], the re-establishment of democracy is complete. I may be permitted to express doubts that in a period of one or two years it would be possible to recover completely from the abuses cf a military dictatorship. Good intentions may have existed, of course, but I refuse to believe that there were no chance mishaps.

The formal political shift must be implemented in fact, and result in a genuine ability and willingness to protect the refugee. Cessation is not warranted where, for example, *de facto* executive authority remains in the hands of the former oppressors:

> The fact that there were "above board" elections in Peru in 1980-81, which sent members of various parties and factions to the parliament, does not prove that the applicant does not have a well-founded fear of returning to his country, which is still, as far as executive authority is concerned, a military dictatorship which tolerates no opposition. It is just another case of old wine in new bottles.

Nor can it be said, that there has truly been a fundamental change of circumstances where the police or military establishments have yet fully to comply with the dictates of democracy and respect for human rights:

> It was argued that the applicant, need no longer be afraid of returning to his homeland as there has been a change in the government since he left. The applicant, however, adduced evidence to show that although the government has changed, members of the Peruvian police and armed forces are still violating human rights and as yet do not appear to be under control by the new government.

In other words, the refugee's right to protection ought not to be compromised simply because progress is being made toward real respect for human rights, even where international scrutiny of that transition is possible. Two mid-1989 judgments of the Immigration and Refugee Board, relating to Poland and Sri Lanka respectively, demonstrate an appropriate concern to see evidence of the real impact of a formal transition of power:

> ... Solidarity calculates that the Communist Party directly or indirectly controls about 900,000 appointments. . . the nomenklatura casts its own shadow in other words, changing the government does not [necessarily] change much. The panel is of the view that the claimant's fear that the changes in Poland are still too uncertain is supported by the documentary evidence.
>
> Although it is alleged that the scale of military confrontation between the Indian Peacekeeping Force and the Tigers has diminished in recent months, there is still an intense rivalry between the Tamil militant groups for the control of the territory and the population. We agree with the points made by counsel, that the normalization process has not yet achieved political stability and peace for Sri Lanka.

Third, the change of circumstances must be shown to be durable. Cessation is not a decision to be taken lightly on the basis of transitory shifts in the political landscape, but should rather be reserved for situations in which there is reason to believe that the positive conversion of the power structure is likely to last. This condition is in keeping with the forward-looking nature of the refugee definition, and avoids the disruption of protection in circumstances where safety may be only a momentary aberration.

The Convention provides for the exemption from cessation based on change of circumstances for pre-1951 refugees who are able to make a case for not returning home based on "compelling reasons arising out of previous persecution". The intention of the drafters was twofold: first, to recognize the legitimacy of the psychological hardship that would be faced by the victims of persecution were they to be returned to the country responsible for their maltreatment; and second, to protect the victims of past atrocities from harm at the hands of private citizens, whose attitudes may not have reformed in tandem with the political structure.

The exemption clause in the Convention is NOT, therefore, structured to provide general humanitarian relief based on factors such as family circumstances or infirmity, but focuses squarely on compelling circumstances which are linked to past persecution. Atle Grahl-Madsen suggests that the existence of a psychological distance between the refugee and her former home, the continued unpopularity in the country of origin of the views or personal characteristics of the refugee, or the severing of familial, social and other linkages between the refugee and her state of origin are the sorts of concerns which warrant exemption from return. In contrast, essentially economic motivations or considerations of personal convenience are not sufficient.

The Canadian legislation adopts these general principles, and extends them to modern day refugees. Insofar as a formal, effective, and enduring change of political structure is found to be in place in the country of origin, therefore, the Board must go on to consider whether the particular refugee continues to suffer the effects of past persecution, in which case cessation should be withheld.

### Persons Who Benefit from Surrogate National or International Protection

Because the Convention is designed to provide protection only to those who truly require it, persons who have successfully obtained surrogate international or national protection are not within the scope of the definition. Like those who have been restored to the protection of their state of nationality or former habitual residence, those with meaningful surrogate protection are deemed to be adequately provided for under international law.

This general category speaks to three distinct situations. First, there are persons who are in receipt of enduring protection or assistance from a specialized agency of the United Nations itself. Second, some refugees may go on to acquire the citizenship of a new state. Third, formally unprotected persons may nonetheless secure the *de facto* protection of a new country on terms substantively similar to those of its nationals. In each of these circumstances, refugee status may be denied or revoked on the basis of the sufficiency of subsisting entitlements.

### Acquisition of a New Nationality

If a refugee cannot resume the protection of her own state, the preferred surrogate is surely the acquisition of citizenship in another country which can effectively ensure her welfare. As was remarked during the drafting of the Convention,

> Both in theory and in practice, naturalization had

> always been considered as bringing refugee status to an end.... [R]efugee status, being abnormal, should not be granted for a day longer than was absolutely necessary, and should come to an end (or, possibly, should never even come into existence if. . . [the refugee) really had the rights and obligations of a citizen of a given country.

Thus, the Convention provides for the cessation of status when the refugee becomes a citizen of her asylum state or of some other country which is able effectively to protect her.

It is a matter of some dispute whether cessation may result from the involuntary acquisition of a new nationality. On the one hand, this was not the intention of the drafters of the Convention. The representative of the Netherlands moved an amendment expressly to recognize the importance of voluntarism in the choice of a new nationality, but was persuaded that the change was not required since the cessation clause

> ... was not concerned with the imposition of nationality by an outside authority, but related to the acquisition by a refugee of a new nationality other than that of the country of persecution. Sub-paragraph 3 was designed to meet the case where a refugee in a particular country of refuge paid a brief visit to another country and took advantage of the facilities available there to acquire the nationality of that country. When such a person returned to the country of refuge, the latter would be faced with the situation of his having acquired a new nationality.

It is clear that delegates to the Conference of Plenipotentiaries did not agree that involuntarily acquired citizenship was cause for cessation and adopted the clause on the understanding that it was restricted to voluntarily secured nationality.

On the other hand, it is true that this clause, unlike the surrounding paragraphs of Article I (C), does not expressly condition cessation on a voluntary act. Too, substantive symmetry with the dual and multiple nationality provisions of Article I(A)( 2) would argue against considerations of voluntarism, Thus, both scholarly opinion and UNHCR recommendations urge that the only relevant issue is the effectiveness of the new nationality, however it came to be acquired. Specifically, the refugee must be able to enter her new state of citizenship, reside there with protection against deportation or exculsion, and enjoy a reasonable expectation that her basic human rights will be fully respected. In such circumstances, adequate surrogate protection exists, and refugee status should logically come to an end.

**Residence with the Rights and Obligations of a National**

This exclusion clause was originally intended simply to bar from international protection all ethnic German refugees from Central and Eastern Europe who had taken up residence in Germany during or following the Second World War. The provision reflected the view that Germany was morally responsible for these migrants, and was in fact meeting their needs by assimilation to its own population, even if they were not always granted formal German nationality. Concern about the diplomatic wisdom of a specific reference to Germany in the Convention led to the formulation of a generally phrased exclusion of ethnically or culturally affiliated residents of a country who receive the same protection as that provided to nationals.

Ironically, this '"politically sensitive" use of general language led to substantial debate in the General Assembly.

The Mexican representative opposed the apparent exclusion of Spanish refugees admitted to his country, or of Spanish Basques in France; the delegate of Saudi Arabia argued more generally that "persons forced to flee to a neighbouring State, the inhabitants of which might have similar racial and cultural characteristics, would be denied the protection both of the Convention and of the High Commissioner's Office". French assurances (hat the clause was aimed only at the German minorities notwithstanding, the original wording was voted down. The revised proposal presented to the Assembly was represented to exclude only "persons involved in mass movements of population due to frontier changes, who possessed the same rights as the inhabitants of the country in which they were currently living", and was further amended to delete any reference to ethnic or cultural kinship, and to focus squarely on the existence of protection genuinely equivalent to that afforded nationals.

Read in this context, exclusion based on *de facto* nationality is truly an exceptional occurrence which implies the effective legal assimilation of the refugee to her host population. Because the clause requires residence in the state willing to confer effective nationality, neither an inchoate right to protection, nor indeed physical presence short of continued residence, is sufficient to warrant exclusion.

Moreover, *de facto* nationality is qualitatively distinct from even long-term residence in a state, since it requires a consequential guarantee of rights to the refugee on terms at least as favourable as those which follow from Convention refugee status. Most critically, the rights of entry and of freedom from removal or expulsion must be clearly conferred and respected, a point emphasized by the Federal Court of Appeal in both *Waclaw Antoni Mihael Hurt v. Minister of Manpower* and Immigration and *Kammy Boun-Leua v. Minister of Employment and Immigration.* As noted in a recent decision to exclude an Iranian with de facto refugee status in Denmark, it must also be determined whether "the claimant enjoys the kinds of rights and protection in [the country of effective nationality] which would bring him within the purview of Section E of Article 1". The Board has since elaborated this requirement to include respect for the claimant's rights under the Convention and the International Bill of Rights, and even "the potential to become a citizen and thus vote in national elections and run for public office". Where these stringent criteria are satisfied, the substance if not the form of a new, surrogate nationality is present, and protection through refugee law is not required.

**Persons Who Do Not Deserve Protection**

The drafters of the Convention were preoccupied to avoid the granting of refugee status to both war criminals and individuals who might jeopardize the internal security of asylum countries. The decision to exclude such persons, even if they are genuinely at risk of persecution in their state of origin, is rooted in both a commitment to the promotion of an international morality and a pragmatic recognition that states are unlikely to agree to be bound by a regime Which requires them to protect undesirable refugees. Relying on the Universal Declaration of Human Rights' prohibition on the granting of asylum to persons liable to prosecution for "non-political crimes or. . . acts contrary to the purposes and principles of the United Nations", the Convention provides for the mandatory exclusion of three classes of persons: those who have committed crimes against peace and security; serious common law criminals; and individuals who have acted in contravention of the principles and purposes of the United Nations.

While the proscription is not subject to any exceptions,

it falls to each contracting state to decide for itself when a refugee claimant is within the scope of an exclusion clause:

> ... in the absence of a world government and of a sovereign international court of justice, that power of discretion, which was an essential safeguard both for the real refugee and for the country of refuge, must, perforce, be left to States. The only-practical solution was to trust the countries which were willing to grant hospitality.

The asylum state need have only "serious reasons for considering" that the applicant is a criminal described in the exclusion clause; there is no requirement that she have been formally charged or convicted, or even that her criminality be capable of establishment "beyond a reasonable doubt" by a judicial procedure. It is enough that the determination authority have "sufficient proof warranting the assumption of [the claimant's] guilt of such a crime"

**Crimes Against Peace and Security**

While the drafters of the Convention were unanimously of the view that war criminals should not be entitled to claim refugee status, there was disagreement on two points. First, the United States argued that countries should be allowed to treat war criminals as refugees, although they should not be compelled to do so. Most representatives, however, were strongly of the view that discretion of this kind could undermine the integrity of refugee status. Second, Germany opposed incorporation of the definition of war criminals derived from the Charter of the International Military Tribunal (the "Nurnberg Principles"), and advocated reference to the "grave breaches" standard of common Article 147 of the Geneva Conventions instead. This met with opposition based on the importance of safeguarding the jurisprudential clarity already achieved by practice under the Nurnberg Principles.

As customarily interpreted, this exclusion clause therefore bars those who commit three distinct types of crime. First, a "crime against peace" comprises the planning of or participation in an unlawful war. Second, a "war crime" involves the violation of a law of war, including the mistreatment of civilians and prisoners of war, or the infliction of unjustified property damage during wartime. Third, a "crime against humanity" consists of fundamentally inhumane conduct, often grounded in political, racial, religious or other bias. Genocide, slavery, torture, and apartheid, are examples of crimes within this category.

An alternative to the plethora of international instruments which now define and describe these crimes against international peace and security has been under construction by the International Law Commission since 1947. Indeed, the drafters of the Convention chose not to elaborate a detailed definition of these crimes partly in deference to the anticipated release of the Commission's *Code of Offences Against the Peace and Security of Mankind.* While still not complete, the draft Code offers a conceptual framework to define crimes within this exclusion clause, and the limited scope of the explanations which may be invoked in relation to them.

The essential nature of a crime against peace and security was elaborated by the Commission in 1987, focusing on the criterion of seriousness:

> These are crimes which affect the very foundations of human society. Seriousness can be deduced either from the nature of the act in question (cruelty, mons trousness, barbarity, etc.), or from the extent of its effects (massiveness, the victims being peoples,

> populations or ethnic groups), or from the motive of the perpetrator (for example, genocide), or from several of these elements.

Intention is a necessary element of such an offence, although some legal experts hold that it may be implied in the case of massive and systematic crimes, such as genocide or apartheid. Because of this *mens rea* requirement, the Commission's draft suggests that three limited exceptions to the general principle of responsibility are available.

In *Zacarias Osorio Cruz* the Immigration Appeal Board allowed the claim of a deserter from the Mexican army, who admitted active participation in approximately twenty politically motivated executions over a five year period. He eventually made a daring escape from his unit due to his "awakening political and moral conscience", and claimed refugee status in Canada. In allowing his claim, the Board did not address the question of whether a crime of this sort could admit of a mistake of law, much less whether the claimant had genuinely "exerted his conscience" prior to engagement in actions properly characterized by the Board as "contrary to the most basic international rules of conduct".

However, this case raises Quite poignantly the issue of whether an additional form of exculpation rooted in utilitarianism is not warranted. The Board placed emphasis on the fact that Osorio Cruz was the first person to shed light on the crimes against humanity being committed by the Mexican army:

> In deserting from the army and telling the whole world, as it had never been told before, the story of the atrocities committed by officers of the Government of Mexico, Mr. Osorio Cruz betrayed his oath of obedience, became a traitor in the eyes of some Mexican authorities by displaying his strong political disagreement and

without a doubt, the worst punishment reserved for prisoners holding unpopular political opinions awaited him. This is the reason for his fear.

While Osorio Cruz' protracted involvement with crimes against humanity may be too egregious to warrant exculpation on any basis, in the case of a less confirmed criminal one might reasonably consider whether the value of disclosure of previously covert inhumane conduct does not offset the general rule against sheltering an admitted criminal. Since the enforcement of international human rights law is dependent on publicity and moral probation, it may be wise judiciously to exonerate individuals who, though culpable themselves, make it possible to end or curtail crimes against peace and security. This position is not, however, thus far accepted in law.

The commentary which accompanies the International Law Commission draft also fails to suggest a specific superior order' exception, although it notes that soldiers or others following commands may invoke the notions coercion or error of law, as defined above. In contrast, the Immigration and Refugee Board accepted the claim of a member of a Ghanaian firing squad involved in politically motivated executions under colour of judicial authority, noting that "the claimant is not a person described in Section F [of] Article 1, because he was a private in the Ghanaian Army and killed people in the line of duty. Because criminal responsibility for actions against peace and security is intended to compel subordinates to question the illegitimate exercise of authority, a "superior order" defence would be counterproductive.

In sum, a crime against peace and security is defined by its seriousness, whether based on the nature of the act itself, the extent of its effects, or the motive of the perpetrator. A person who commits such an act is culpable unless a strictly construed exception based on self-defence, coercion, or error of law can be established. Moreover, all of the recognized exceptions to responsibility for crimes against peace and security are inoperative if the facts invoked constitute a breach of a peremptory norm of international law, originate in a fault of the perpetrator, or result in the sacrifice of a greater interest than that protected.

The last question to be addressed is the degree of involvement required to justify criminal liability. While mere presence at the scene of a crime may not be actionable, exclusion is warranted "when the evidence establishes that the individual in question personally ordered, incited, assisted or otherwise participated in the persecution..." In Fernando Alfonso Naredo Arduengo, for example, the Immigration Appeal Board disqualified the Chilean applicants who had been employed by that country's secret police:

> Mr. and Mrs. Naredo were members of different four or five mean teams engaged in surveillance, arrests and interrogations, which involved torture and beatings. Both claimed to have been assigned to stand guard and take notes, denying that they personally beat or tortured their victims. Mr. Naredo claims to have participated in eighteen to twenty such operations, ten leading to death.... [T]heir actions so clearly an abuse of human right's, set them outside those who can properly seek asylum.

The same holds true for those who make it possible for others to engage in crimes against peace and security:

> That Mr. Giraud did not kill anyone directly is not to his credit. He prepared them for death, which in my view makes aim culpable.... Mr. Giraud has, in my view, committed a... crime against humanity.

### Serious Non-Political Crimes

The common law criminality exclusion disallows the claims of persons who are liable to sanctions in another state for having committed a genuine, serious crime, and who seek to escape legitimate criminal liability by claiming refugee status. This exclusion clause is not a means of by passing ordinary criminal due process for acts committed in a state of refuge, nor a pretext for ignoring the protection needs of those whose transgressions abroad are of a comparatively minor nature. Rather, it is simply a means of bringing refugee law into line with the basic principles of extradition law, by ensuring that important fugitives from justice are not able to avoid the jurisdiction of a state in which they may lawfully face punishment:

> Article 14 of the Universal Declaration of Human Rights was concerned with the right of asylum, and its second paragraph constituted a proviso to the general provision of the first paragraph. That second paragraph seemed... to be intended to apply to persons who were fugitives from prosecution in another country for non-political crimes, and the effect would seem to be that the provisions of article 14 would not override specific extradition obligations.... [T]he Convention mentioned neither the right of asylum nor the principle of extradition. In that connexion, the action of States was governed by treaties relating specifically to extradition, and it would therefore be for states to take appropriate action in any given case in the light of their obligations under such treaties.

In view of this narrow purpose, the common law criminality clause is subject to several important constraints.

First, it follows from the linkage to extradition that the only allegations of criminality which are relevant to the application of this clause are those which involve acts committed outside a country of refuge, whether in the country of origin or while in transit to an asylum state. As noted by the Canadian representative, just prior to the vote on this clause,

> ... the issue turned on the temporal element, namely, whether a person had committed a crime outside the territory of the receiving country before he had applied for the status of refugee.

Criminal activity in a state of refuge, on the other hand, is appropriately adjudicated through due process of law, with recourse to expulsion or return if the refugee is consequently found to pose a security 'risk.

Second, the extradition-based rationale for the exclusion clause requires that the criminal offence be justiciable in the country in which it was committed. Insofar as the claimant has served her sentence, been acquitted of the charges, benefited from an amnesty or otherwise met her obligations under the criminal law, she would be at no risk "of extradition, and should not be excluded from refugee status. As Paul Weis has observed.

> It is... difficult to see why a person who before becoming a refugee, has been convicted of a serious crime and has served his sentence should forever be debarred from refugee status. Such a rule would seem to run counter to the generally accepted principle of penal law that a person who has been punished for an offence should suffer no further prejudice on account of the offence committed.

Indeed, delegates to the Conference on Territorial Asylum were able to agree that the criminality exclusion should bar only the claims of persons believed to be "still liable to prosecution or punishment".

Third, the drafters recognized the seriousness of refusing to protect a person at risk of persecution, and therefore chose to limit the criminality exception to persons at risk of prosecution or punishment for a serious crime within the realm of extraditable offences. In pressing for a narrowly interpreted exclusion, the British delegate argued against simple incorporation of the non-political crime exclusion from the Universal Declaration of Human Rights:

> But what was meant by considering that a person fell within a category of prosecutions? A person who was prosecuted and convicted would certainly seem to fall within that category. As it stood, therefore, clause (b) would include refugees who had committed a crime, no matter how trivial... provided it was not a political crime, and would thus automatically exclude them from the benefits of the Convention. It must be obvious to all that such a proposition was untenable.

# 9

# INDIAN POLICY ON REFUGEE

> "If this Republic is to remain the land of the free and continue to grow in strength and usefulness, both the native and foreign born, who exercise the right of suffrage, must one and all be thoroughly schooled in the meaning of democracy and in the duties and obligations of the citizen.
>
> The Republic cannot endure permanently half American and half hyphenated."
>
> —*Gen. John J. Pershing*

## Indian Practice of Asylum and Non-refoulement

Asylum is the protection which a state grants on its territory or in some other-place under the control of certain of its organs, to a person who comes to seek it. To speak of refugees is to speak of asylum, the very condition of their existence. The international law on asylum, is comparatively new and it took its present from only little more than a century ago. Art. 14 of the Universal Declaration of Human Rights lays down the fundamental rule of asylum which may not be invoked in the case of persecution genuinely arising from non-political crimes or from acts contrary to the purposes and principles of the United Nations.

Here it is very much important to note that the term

'asylum' has no universally accepted definition. So, generally it is used in the sense of admission to the territory of a state, and a distinction is made between admission which is granted as an emergency measure, guaranteeing refuge of a temporary nature only, and admission which encompasses the more durable aspect involved in the grant of a permanent right to settle .31 The fundamental principle governing admission is that of non-rejection at the frontier, which has been considered in aspect of the more general principal of non-refoulement. The rule of non-refoulement thus incorporates the obligation to refrain from forcibly returning a refugee to a country where he is likely to suffer political persecution.

This principle of non-refoulement constitutes the very basis of the institution of asylum and an essential guarantee for the asylee that he would receive the protection—defined in Art. 14 of the Universal Declaration; in some cases it would be tantamount to an asylee's right to life.' India has all along followed the principle of nonrefoulement. The Government of India allowed the unending streams of refugees in utter distress entry into India and gave solace and comfort. Evidence of India's ancient history shows that once the king granted shelter-to any individual it was his sacred duty to protect the refugee at all times."

In 1959 when Dalai Lama of Tibet crossed over to India along with nearly 13,000 of his followers-the Government of India granted the political asylum to all those people on humanitarian ground. But it made the asylum conditional upon the Dalai Lama residing in India peacefully and not engaging himself-or his followers in political activities. The condition imposed by the Government of India was at per with the international norm. The refugees have a general obligation to respect the laws and regulations of the country in which they find themselves. In this respect they are not on different footing from the citizens of the country, or for that matter, any other foreigner. This obligation includes a duty to refrain from engaging in subversive activities directed against their country of origin, such as armed insurrection.

Again in 1971, when 10 million people crossed over in its territory from the erstwhile East Pakistan, the Government of India granted them temporary asylum on humanitarian ground. Mrs. Indira Gandhi, the then Prime Minister, in her statement in Lok Sabha on May 24, 1971 on "situation in Bangladesh" made it very clear that-

> "Relief can not be perpetual, or permanent, and we do not wish it to be so. Conditions must be created to stop my further influx of refugees and to ensure their early return under credible guarantees for their future safety and well-being".

She further added that-

> "I hope this Parliament, our country and our people will be ready to accept the necessary hardships so that we can discharge our responsibilities to our own people as well as to the millions, who have fled from a reign of terror to take temporary-refuge here".

In reply to a reporter's question in Calcutta on 5 June, 1971, Mrs. Indira Gandhi clearly stated that the refugees would be looked after on a temporary basis. They needed to be treated as foreigners to be repatriated to Bangladesh for which conditions should have to be created within that country. As she stated further

> "they have to go back. They are certainly not going to stay here permanently. I am determined to send them back".

In view of the above, the status of asylum given to the refugees from East Bengal must be deemed to be provisional or temporary asylum. In all other subsequent cases viz.; in the case of Tamil refugees from Sri Lanka, in the case of Chakma refugees from Bangladesh-India followed 'the same practice of 'temporary asylum'.

Article III of the Bangkok Principles of 1966 provides the provision on this temporary or provisional- asylum.

*Article III lays down that:*

"1. A state has the sovereign right to grant or refuse asylum in its territory to a refugee.

2. The exercise of the right to grant, such asylum to, a refugee shall be respected by all other states and shall not be regarded as an unfriendly act.

3. No one seeking asylum in accordance with these principles should, except for overriding reasons of national security or safeguarding the populations, be subjected to measures such as rejection at the frontier, return or expulsion which would result in compelling him to return to or remain in a territory if there is a well-founded fear of persecution endangering his life, physical integrity or liberty in that territory.

4. In cases where a state decides to apply any of the above-mentioned measures to a person seeking asylum, it should grant provisional asylum under such conditions as it may deem appropriate, to enable the person thus endangered to seek asylum in another country".

So, India granted 'provisional asylum' or 'temporary asylum' to the refugees as per the present international norm'. However, even though India accepted the principle of nonrefoulement as including non-rejection at the frontier under the 'Bangkok Principles' of 1966, it did not observe that principle in its practice. The actual practice is that India deals with the question of admission of refugees and their stay, until they are officially accorded refugee status, under legislations which deal with foreigners who voluntarily leave their homes in normal circumstances.

The chief legislation for the regulation of foreigners is the Foreigners Act, 1946, which deals with the matters of entry of foreigners in India, their presence therein and their departure therefrom. *Para 3(1) of the Foreigners Order, 1948* lays down the power to grant or refuse permission to a foreigner to enter India. This provision lays down a general obligation that no foreigner should enter India without the authorization of the authority having jurisdiction over such entry points.

In case of persons who do not fulfil certain obligations of entry, the Sub-Para 2 of the Para-3 of the Order authorizes the civil authority to refuse the leave to enter India. The main condition is that unless exempted, every foreigner should be in possession of a valid passport or visa to enter India. If refugees contravene any of these provisions they are liable to prosecution and thereby to the deportation proceedings. Here it is noteworthy that India has not established any refugee determination criteria or procedure and it is the union Cabinet which decides on the kind of protection to be provided to the entrants.

Since, there is no legislation and legal procedure for determining their status, so they are being treated as *'alien refugees'* under Entry 17, List 1, Sch. 7, of the Indian Constitution. The difference between an alien and an alien refugee is that the latter is given residential permit exempting from certain conditionalities of stay of a foreigner depending on his political refugee status in India, whereas an alien or foreigner has to show valid grounds for his stay if he intends to stay more than ninety days in India.

So, the natural consequence is that refugees have to be treated under the law applicable to aliens in India, unless it makes a specific provision as it did in the case of Ugandan refugees (of Indian origin) when it passed the Foreigners From Uganda Order 1972. The Registration Act of 1939 deals with the registration of foreigners entering, being present in, and departing from India. Besides this, there are : (i) the Passport (Entry into India) Act 1920 and the Passport Act of 1967, dealing with the powers of the Government to impose conditions of particularly with regard to the right to possession of a passport for entry into India; and the issue of passports and travel documents to regulate the departure from India of citizens of India and applies in certain cases to others too, respectively.

**Treatment of Persons Granted Asylum in India**

This may be discussed under these heads

(a) National treatment, (b) Treatment that is accorded to foreigners, 'and (c) Special treatment.

***(a) National Treatment***

(i) Equal Protection of Law—Article 14 of the Indian Constitution guarantees the right that state shall not deny to any person equality before the law or the equal protection of the law within the territory of India. This right is available to all persons including non-citizens. So, as per the provision of this Article, State would not discriminate a refugee against other refugees of same class regarding any benefits or rights they enjoy by virtue of their refugee status.

(ii) Religious Freedom-Article 25 of the Indian

Constitution provides that subject to public order, morality and health and to the other provisions of the constitution, all persons are equally entitled to freedom of conscience and the right freely to profess, practice and propagate religion.

(iii) Right to Liberty, etc.-Article 21 of the Indian Constitution guarantees the right to life and personal liberty of all persons. A person is further guaranteed protection against arbitrary arrest and detention, and free access to the courts. Here it is important to note that the right to life, personal liberty and free access to the courts (under Arts. 21 and 22) have been extended to every person irrespective of the fact whether the person concerned is an alien, refugee, or a citizen of India. His free access to the courts is assured under Articles 32 and 226 of the Constitution equality and protection of law, right to practice his own religion, the right to life and personal liberty. So, as desired in Art. 16 of the 1951 Refugee Convention, a refugee has free access to the courts of law in India as permitted under the Constitution.

(iv) Right to Social Security-Regarding right to Social Security, there is no special provision on social security in any Indian legislations, but non-citizens in India enjoy social security—equally with citizens.

(v) Educational Rights-India has been providing free primary education to all recognised refugees, although there is no legal guarantee for the enjoyment of that facility as a matter of right. As for higher education, only Tibetan refugees "enjoy that privilege.

### *(b) Treatment that is Accorded to Foreigners*

(i) Right to employment or profession:

Among the main rights of concern to the refugee is that of free access to employment, which in practice means the right to an independent existence. In the case of wage earning employment, Article 17 of the 1951 Convention provides that the contracting state shall accord to refugees lawfully staying in their territory the most favourable treatment accorded to aliens. Art. 17 further invites contracting states to give sympathetic consideration to assimilating the rights of all refugees with regard to wage-earning employment to those of nationals. The provisions of Articles 18 and 19 concerning self-employment and the liberty of profession do not go so far. They merely refer to "treatment as favourable as possible and in any extent, not less favourable than that accorded to aliens generally".

However, so far the Indian practice is concerned in this field, no foreigner in India has a right to a wage-earning employment, self-employment or profession, but he can do that with the permission of the Government of India. When it comes to the question of refugees, there are in fact no restriction on wage-earning or self-employment but they are not usually allowed to undertake any work since India has a large population of unemployed citizens. Instead, refugees are 'provided with some subsistence allowance and ration by the Union Government of India. Exception to this are Tibetans who are allowed to engage themselves in wage-earning employment in agriculture, agro-industries and handicrafts specially set Lip for their rehabilitation. They are also engaged in small business such as selling, of handicrafts and winter clothes.

(ii) Freedom of movement and residence:

Article 26 of the 1951 Convention proclaims the right of refugees to choose their place of residence 'and to move freely within the territory of the country concerned. In India this freedom of movement and residence is available to all refugees, subject to the restrictions necessary for the safety of India or its international relations. The refugees who could afford to live on their own are allowed to live wherever they want and they are given freedom to move within India subject to conditions such as national security or public order. In case of large number of refugees such as Chakmas in Tripura and Sri Lankan Tamils in Tamil Nadu, their right to freedom of movement and residence is hampered by the fact that they are totally dependent on the Government. They are therefore, confined to camps. When they need to go out from the camps they need to take permission of the camp authorities.

(iii) Right to housing-The requirement of Art. 21 of the 1951 Refugee Convention in connection with 'housing' is fulfilled, and while the refugees are free to live in refugee camps, there is no rule to prohibit them from residing in private houses if they can afford. Many Afghan and Sri Lankan refugees are residing in private houses in Delhi and Madras respectively.

(iv) Right to form association- Art. 15 of the 1951 Convention Relating to the Status of Refugees lays down that as regards non-political and non-profit making associations and trade unions the contracting states shall accord to refugees lawfully staying in their territory the most favorable treatment accorded to nationals of a foreign country, in the same circumstances.

In India, like foreigners, refugees too enjoy the right to form peaceful associations. Burmese and Chakma refugee communities have formed student and welfare refugee associations. In Tripura, Chittagong Hill Tracts Jumma Refugees' Welfare Association headed by Mr. Upendralal Chakma is actively engaged in the day to day welfare activities of the Chakma refugees.

(v) Property Rights-Art. 13 of the 1951 Convention states that the contracting states shall accord to a refugee treatment as favourable as possible and,, in any event, not less favourable than that accorded to aliens generally in the same circumstances, as regards the acquisition of movable and immovable property and other rights pertaining thereto, and to leases and other contracts-relating to movable and immovable property.

However, in India this right has not been accorded to the refugees. Even after three decades of their rehabilitation, Tibetans do not enjoy any property rights over the agricultural lands and houses which they were allowed to use on lease.

***(c) Special Treatment***

(i) Exemption from penalties:

Art. 3(1) of the 1951 Refugee Convention provides that "the contracting state shall not impose penalties, on account of their illegal entry or presence on refugees who coming directly from a territory. Where their life or freedom was threatened.... enter or are present in their territory without authorization, provided they present themselves without delay to the authorities and show good cause for their illegal entry or presence." This is one area where India is very apathetic towards refugees. Under section 14 of the Foreigners Act, 1946 a foreigner is liable - to the punishment with imprisonment for a term which may extend to five years and is also liable to fine. Due to lack of a procedure for considering asylum claims, all individual asylum-seekers who entered illegally or stayed in India without authorization were persecuted and punished under this section. However, in case of large-scale influx, India has always acted according to the principle laid down in the Refugee Convention and has not imposed penalties on the refugees.

Indeed, the question remains with respect of asylum-seekers of other national groups determined to be refugees under the mandate of UNHCR. Differential treatment already exists in the way the host government treats individual refugees recognized under the UNHCR mandate and those of man influxes from neighbouring states. With respect to the former, their non-recognition before the law and uncertain status renders them open to risk of penalization for illegal entry and expulsion while there is a: greater measure of fundamental protection with respect of the latter.

(ii) Identity and travel documents

Since refugees do not enjoy the protection of the government of their country of origin, they can not claim a national passport. Only the authorities of the country of residence can make good this deficiency by issuing them a suitable travel documents. Since, however, this document is of no value unless it is recognised internationally, each of the agreements concluded after the First World War to assist various groups of refugees make explicit reference to it. The 1951 Convention was no exception to this rule. Article 28 of the Convention provides that:

The Contracting States shall issue to refugees lawfully staying in their territory travel documents for the purpose of travel outside their territory unless compelling reason of national security or public order otherwise require".

In India, all refugees who are recognized so were given identification certificates showing their refugee status. But, as regards travel documents; no refugee has so far had a privilege of getting travel documents except Tibetan refugees. Tibetan refugees can even travel to foreign countries and come back to India on the basis of the such identification paper.

**Co-operation with UNHCR**

India, for the first time, established its formal relationship with the United Nations High Commissioner for Refugees in 1969 for rehabilitating Tibetan refugees in India. When the High Commissioner visited India in July 1963, India expressed its interest in receiving assistance from the Office of the United Nations High Commissioner for Refugees for Tibetan refugees. UNHCR made available some funds from the proceedings of the sale of "All Star Festival" record. Since a pre-requisite for such assistance was the proper supervision of UNHCR funds and careful coordination of international efforts, Indian Government agreed that the presence of an on-the-spot UNHCR representative was desirable. A Branch office of UNHCR was officially opened in Delhi on February 1,1969. In co-operation with India

UNHCR undertook new projects and consolidated old ones in the fields of agricultural settlements, housing for the aged lamas, and medical facilities. Thus, a close working relationship between UNHCR and India was established by the time India got involved in providing emergency relief to Bangladesh refugees.

Here it is worthwhile to mention that to cope with the refugee influx from East Pakistan, on 23 April 1971 India called upon the UN family to assist in bringing relief in order to meet massive refugee problem. Responding to India's call, the Secretary General of the United Nations appointed the United Nations High Commissioner for Refugees as the Co-ordinator of assistance, and in June, a unit (UNEPRO) was created in East Pakistan itself to relieve the plight of civilians in that territory. In May 1971, the High Commissioner sent a fact finding Commission to, India. The Commission's report stated that two matters were of utmost importance: urgent, relief measures and the promotion of voluntary repatriation. The assistance programme ran from May 1971 to February 1972. It directly involved UNICEF, WHO, FAO and WFP to co-ordinate fundraising and assistance activities. The High Commissioner for Refugees was entrusted with the work of liaison with the Government of India and the governments which contributed to the relief efforts in cash and kind.

After 1972, UNHCR Branch office In Delhi concentrated on resettlement, projects for Tibetan, refugees again. But in. 1975 UNHCR suddenly wound up its projects in India and closed its Delhi Branch office for no reason. Again in 1479 UNHCR requested the Government of India to reopen its Branch Office in Delhi. India did not give permission to that effect, but agreed to allow a UNHCR representative to function as the "UNHCR component of the United Nations

Development Programme (UNDP)" in New Delhi. However, in 1981 the Government of India allowed the UNHCR to re-open its office in New Delhi after a significant number of refugees had arrived from Afghanistan and Iran. But it imposed that the UNHCR must function under the banner of the UNDP.

A controversy raised in 1984 when the UNHCR granted refugee status to three Delhi-based officials of the Afghan Airlines Anna.[39] The Indian position has been that 'refugee status' cannot be granted by New Delhi-based U.N. officials without the approval of the Government of India to an alien within the Indian territory. India also objected to the UN officials granting international protection to three members of the Afghan soccer feam who defected in Delhi while returning from Beijing after participating in a tournament.

However, despite the absence of a formally strong relationship India has a good rapport with UNHCR and it cooperates and assists the later in resolving international refugee problem. In practice, the UNHCR tactfully avoids confrontation and tries to achieve practical results through conciliation. This style is very evident in the manner in which the UNHCR has been operating in New Delhi under the Umbrella of UNDP. Recently, India has become the Member of the Executive Committee of the United Nations 'High Commissioner for Refugees Programme. So, it is hoped that the relation between the two will improve further.

# 10

# Conclusion

> "Everyone has the right to seek and to enjoy in other countries asylum from persecution."
>
> —*UDHR, Article 14*

After having a thorough description of refugee problem and their basic human rights, we will present the entire scenario in this concluding chapter.

Under the United Nations Convention Relating to the Status of Refugees from 1951, a refugee is a person who (according to the formal definition in article 1A of this Convention), "owing to a well-founded fear of being persecuted for reasons of race, religion, nationality, membership of a particular social group, or political opinion, is outside the country of his nationality, and is unable to or, owing to such fear, is unwilling to avail himself of the protection of that country". The concept of a refugee was expanded by the Convention's 1967 Protocol and by regional conventions in Africa and Latin America to include persons who had fled war or other violence in their home country.

Refugees were defined as a legal group n response to the large numbers of people fleeing Eastern Europe following World War II. The lead international agency coordinating refugee protection is the Office of the United Nations High

Commissioner for Refugees (UNHCR), which counted 8,400,000 refugees worldwide at the beginning of 2006. This was the lowest number since 1980. The major exception is the 4,600,000 Palestinian refugees under the authority of the United Nations Relief and Works Agency for Palestine Refugees in the Near East (UNRWA), who are the only group to be granted refugee status to the descendants of refugees according to the above definition.

The U.S. Committee for Refugees and Immigrants gives the world total as 62,000,000 refugees and estimates there are over 34,000,000 displaced by war, including internally displaced persons, who remain within the same national borders. The majority of refugees who leave their country seek asylum in countries neighboring their country of nationality. The "durable solutions" to refugee populations, as defined by UNHCR and governments, are: voluntary repatriation to the country of origin; local integration into the country of asylum; and resettlement to a third country.

As of December 31, 2005, the largest source countries of refugees are Afghanistan, Iraq, Myanmar, Sudan, and the Palestinian Territories. The country with the largest number of IDPs is Sudan, with over 5 million. As of 2006, with 800,000 refugees and IDPs, Azerbaijan had the highest per capita IDP population in the world.

The concept of the meaning that a person who fled into a holy place could not be harmed without inviting divine retribution, was understood by the ancient Greeks and ancient Egyptians. However, the right to seek asylum in a church or other holy place, was first codified in law by King Ethelbert of Kent in about 600 A.D. Similar laws were implemented throughout Europe in the Middle Ages. The related concept of political exile also has a long history: Ovid was sent to Tomis and Voltaire was exiled to England. Through the 1648 Peace of Westphalia, nations recognized each others' sovereignty. However, it was not until the advent of romantic nationalism in late eighteenth century Europe that nationalism became prevalent enough that the phrase "country of nationality" became meaningful and people crossing borders were required to provide identification.

The term "refugee" is sometimes applied to people who may have fit the definition, if the 1951 Convention was applied retroactively. There are many candidates. For example, after the Edict of Fontainebleau in 1685 outlawed Protestantism in France, hundreds of thousands of Huguenots fled to England, the Netherlands, Switzerland, South Africa, Germany and Prussia. Repeated waves of pogroms swept Eastern Europe, propelling mass Jewish emigration (more than 2 million Russian Jews emigrated in the period 1881–1920). Since the 19th century, an exodus by the large portion of Muslim peoples (who are termed "Muhacir" under a general definition) from the Balkans, Caucasus, Crimea and Crete, took refuge in present-day Turkey and moulded the country's fundamental features. The Balkan Wars of 1912–1913 caused 800,000 people to leave their homes. Various groups of people were officially designated refugees beginning in World War I.

### *Under the League of Nations*

The first international coordination on refugee affairs was by the League of Nations' High Commission for Refugees. The Commission, led by Fridtjof Nansen, was set up in 1921 to assist the approximately 1,500,000 persons who fled the Russian Revolution of 1917 and the subsequent civil war (1917–1921), most of them aristocrats fleeing the Communist government. In 1923, the mandate of the Commission was expanded to include the more than one million Armenians who left Turkish Asia Minor in 1915 and 1923 due to a series of events now known as the Armenian Genocide. Over the next several years, the mandate was expanded to include Assyrians and Turkish refugees. In all of these cases, a refugee was defined as a person in a group for which the League of Nations had approved a mandate, as opposed to a person to whom a general definition applied.

The 1923 population exchange between Greece and Turkey involved some two million people, most forcibly made refugees and *de jure* denaturalized from homelands of centuries or millennia, in a treaty promoted and overseen by the international community as part of the Treaty of Lausanne.

The U.S. Congress passed the Emergency Quota Act in 1921, followed by the Immigration Act of 1924. The Immigration Act of 1924 was aimed at further restricting the Southern and Eastern Europeans, especially Jews, Italians and Slavs, who had begun to enter the country in large numbers beginning in the 1890s. Most of the European refugees (principally Jews and Slavs) fleeing the Stalin, Nazis and World War II were barred from coming to the United States.

In 1930, the Nansen International Office for Refugees was established as a successor agency to the Commission. Its most notable achievement was the Nansen passport, a passport for refugees, for which it was awarded the 1938 Nobel Peace Prize. The Nansen Office was plagued by inadequate funding, rising numbers of refugees and the refusal by League members to let the Office assist their own citizens. Regardless, it managed to convince fourteen nations to sign the Refugee Convention of 1933, a weak human right instrument, and assist over one million refugees.

The rise of Nazism led to such a severe rise in refugees from Germany that in 1933 the League created a High Commission for Refugees Coming from Germany. On July 4, 1936 an agreement was signed under League auspices that defined refugee coming from Germany as "any person who was settled in that country, who does not possess any nationality other than German nationality, and in respect of whom it is established that in law or in fact he or she does not enjoy the protection of the Government of the Reich" (article 1). The mandate of this High Commission was subsequently expanded to include persons from Austria and Sudetenland. 150,000 Czechs were displaced after October 1, 1938, when the German army entered the border regions of Czechoslovakia surrendered in accordance with the Munich Agreement.

On 31 December 1938, both the Nansen Office and High Commission were dissolved and replaced by the Office of the High Commissioner for Refugees under the Protection of the League. This coincided with the flight of several hundred thousand Spanish Republicans to France after their loss to the Nationalists in 1939 in the Spanish Civil War.

### *World War II and UNHCR*

The conflict and political instability during World War II led to massive amounts of forced migration (see World War II evacuation and expulsion). By the end of World War II, Europe had more than 40 million refugees. In 1943, the Allies created the United Nations Relief and Rehabilitation Administration (UNRRA) to provide aid to areas liberated from Axis powers, including parts of Europe and China. This included returning over seven miliion refugees, then commonly referred to as displaced persons or DPs, to their country of origin and setting up displaced persons camps for one million refugees who refused to be repatriated.

In the last months of World War II some five million German civilians from the German provinces of East Prussia, Pomerania and Silesia fled the onslaught of the Red Army and became refugees in Mecklenburg, Brandenburg and Saxony. After the capitulation of the Wehrmacht in May 1945 the Allies occupied Germany in the borders as they were on 31 December 1937, as agreed to in the Berlin declaration of 5 June 1945. Since the spring of 1945 the Poles had been forcefully expelling the remaining German population in a program of ethnic cleansing. When the Allies met in Potsdam on 17 July 1945 at the Potsdam Conference, a chaotic refugee situation faced the occupying powers. On 2 August 1945, they established the Potsdam protocol. Article IX placed one fourth of Germany's territory under provisional Polish administration and Article XIII ordered that the remaining German populations in Poland, Czechoslovakia and Hungary be transferred West in an "orderly and humane" manner.

Although not approved by Allies at Potsdam, hundreds of thousands of ethnic German living in Yugoslavia and Romania were deported to slave labour in the Soviet Union, to Allied-occupied Germany, and subsequently to the German Democratic Republic, Austria and the Federal Republic of Germany. This entailed the largest population transfer in history. In all 15 million Germans were affected, and more than two million perished during the expulsion of the German population. Between the end of World War II and the erection of the Berlin Wall in 1961, more than 563,700 refugees from East Germany traveled to West Germany for asylum from the Soviet occupation.

During the same period, millions of former Russian citizens were forcefully repatriated against their will into the USSR. On 11 February 1945, at the conclusion of the Yalta Conference, the United States and United Kingdom signed a Repatriation Agreement with the USSR. The interpretation of this Agreement resulted in the forcible repatriation of all Soviets regardless of their wishes. When the war ended in May 1945, British and U.S. civilian authorities ordered their military forces in Europe to deport to the Soviet Union millions of former residents of the USSR, including numerous persons who had left Russia and established different citizenship many years before. The forced repatriation operations took place from 1945 to 1947.

At the end of the World War II, there were more than 5 million "displaced persons" from the Soviet Union in the Western Europe. About 3 million had been forced laborers (Ostarbeiters) in Germany and occupied territories. The Soviet POWs and the Vlasov men were put under the jurisdiction of SMERSH (Death to Spies). Of the 5.7 million Soviet prisoners of war captured by the Germans, 3.5 million had died while in German captivity by the end of the war. The survivors on their return to the USSR were treated as traitors (see Order No. 270). Over 1.5 million surviving Red Army soldiers imprisoned by the Germans were sent to the Gulag.

Poland and Soviet Ukraine conducted population exchanges – Poles that resided east of the established Poland-Soviet border were deported to Poland (ca. 2,100,000 persons) (see Repatriation of Poles) and Ukrainians that resided west of the established Poland-Soviet Union border were deported to Soviet Ukraine. Population transfer to Soviet Ukraine occurred from September 1944 to May 1946 (ca. 450,000 persons) (see Repatriation of Ukrainians). Some Ukrainians (ca. 200,000 persons) left southeast Poland more or less voluntarily (between 1944 and 1945).

The UNRRA was shut down in 1947, at which time it was taken over by the newly instituted International Refugee

Organization. While the handover was originally planned to take place at the beginning of 1947, it did not occur until July 1947. The International Refugee Organization was a temporary organization of the United Nations (UN), which itself had been founded in 1945, with a mandate to largely finish the UNRRA's work of repatriating or resettling European refugees. It was dissolved in 1952 after resettling about one million refugees. The definition of a refugee at this time was an individual with either a Nansen passport or a "Certificate of Eligibility" issued by the International Refugee Organization.

### *UNHCR*

Headquartered in Geneva, Switzerland, the Office of the United Nations High Commissioner for Refugees (UNHCR) (established December 14, 1950) protects and supports refugees at the request of a government or the United Nations and assists in their return or resettlement. All refugees in the world are under the UNHCR mandate except Palestinian Arabs who fled the future Jewish state between 1947 and 1948 (see below). However, Palestinians who fled the Palestinian territories after 1948 (for example, during the 1967 six day war) are under the jurisdiction of the UNHCR.

UNHCR provides protection and assistance not only to refugees, but also to other categories of displaced or needy people. These include asylum seekers, refugees who have returned home but still need help in rebuilding their lives, local civilian communities directly affected by the movements of refugees, stateless people and so-called internally displaced people (IDPs). IDPs are civilians who have been forced to flee their homes, but who have not reached a neighboring country and therefore, unlike refugees, are not protected by international law and may find it hard to receive any form of assistance. As the nature of war has changed in the last few decades, with more and more internal conflicts replacing interstate wars, the number of IDPs has increased significantly to an estimated 5 million people worldwide. It succeeded the earlier International Refugee Organization and the even earlier United Nations Relief and Rehabilitation Administration (which itself succeeded the League of Nations' Commissions for Refugees).

UNHCR was awarded the Nobel Peace Prize in 1954 and 1981. The agency is mandated to lead and co-ordinate international action to protect refugees and resolve refugee problems worldwide. Its primary purpose is to safeguard the rights and well-being of refugees. It strives to ensure that everyone can exercise the right to seek asylum and find safe refuge in another State, with the option to return home voluntarily, integrate locally or to resettle in a third country.

Many celebrities are associated with the agency as UNHCR Goodwill Ambassadors, currently including Angelina Jolie, Giorgio Armani and others. The individual who has raised the most money in benefit performances and volunteer work on behalf of UNHCR was Luciano Pavarotti.

UNHCR's mandate has gradually been expanded to include protecting and providing humanitarian assistance to what it describes as other persons "of concern," including internally-displaced persons (IDPs) who would fit the legal definition of a refugee under the 1951 Refugee Convention and 1967 Protocol, the 1969 Organization for African Unity Convention, or some other treaty if they left their country, but who presently remain in their country of origin. UNHCR thus has missions in Colombia, Democratic Republic of the Congo, Serbia and Montenegro and Côte d'Ivoire to assist and provide services to IDPs. Asia – 8,603,600 Africa – 5,169,300 Europe – 3,666,700 Latin America and Caribbean – 2,513,000 North America – 716,800 Oceania – 82,500.

**Asylum Seekers**

According to international refugee law, a refugee is someone who seeks refuge in a foreign country because of war and violence, or out of fear of persecution. The United States recognizes persecution "on account of race, religion, nationality, political opinion, or membership in a particular social group" as grounds for seeking asylum. Until a request for refuge has been accepted, the person is referred to as an *asylum seeker*. Only after the recognition of the asylum seeker's protection needs, he or she is officially referred to as a refugee and enjoys refugee status, which carries certain rights and obligations according to the legislation of the receiving country. The practical determination of whether a person is a refugee or not is most often left to certain government agencies within the host country.

This can lead to a situation where the country will neither recognize the refugee status of the asylum seekers nor see them as legitimate migrants and treat them as illegal aliens. On the other hand, fraudulent requests in an environment of lax enforcement could lead to improper classification as refugee, resulting in the diversion of resources from those with a genuine need.

The percentage of asylum/refugee seekers who do not meet the international standards of special-needs refugee, and for whom resettlement is deemed proper, varies from country to country. Failed asylum applicants are most often deported, sometimes after imprisonment or detention, as in the United Kingdom. A claim for asylum may also be made onshore, usually after making an unauthorized arrival. Some governments are tolerant and accepting of onshore asylum claims; other governments arrest or detain those who attempt to seek asylum; sometimes while processing their claims.

Non-governmental organizations concerned with refugees and asylum seekers have pointed out difficulties for displaced persons to seek asylum in industrialized countries. As their immigration policy often focuses on the fight of irregular migration and the strengthening of border controls it deters displaced persons from entering territory in which they could lodge an asylum claim. The lack of opportunities to legally access the asylum procedures can force asylum seekers to undertake often expensive and hazardous attempts at illegal entry.

Concerns over arbitrariness in asylum adjudication in the United States have led some commentators to describe the process as refugee roulette; that is, a system in which the identity of the adjudicator, rather than the strength of the asylum seeker's claim, is the determining factor in winning an asylum claim.

**Refugee Resettlement**

Resettlement involves the assisted movement of refugees who are unable to return home to safe third countries. The UNHCR has traditionally seen resettlement as the least preferable of the "durable solutions" to refugee situations. However, in April 2000 the then UN High Commissioner for Refugees, Sadako Ogata, stated:

> "Resettlement can no longer be seen as the least-preferred durable solution; in many cases it is the *only* solution for refugees."
>
> *—Sadako Ogata,*
>
> *UN High Commissioner for Refugees, April 2000*

| *State* | *Quota (2001)* | *Year established* |
|---|---|---|
| United States | 80,000 | 1980 |
| Canada | 11,000 | 1978 |

| | | |
|---|---|---|
| Australia | 15,000 | Unknown |
| Norway | 1,500 | Unknown |
| Sweden | 1,375 | 1950 |
| New Zealand | 750 | 1979 |
| Finland | 750 | 1979 |
| Denmark | 517 | 1989 |
| Netherlands | 500 | 1984 |

UNHCR referred more than 121,000 refugees for consideration for resettlement in 2008. This was the highest number for 15 years. In 2007, 98,999 people were referred. UNHCR referred 33,512 refugees from Iraq, 30,388 from Burma/Myanmar and 23,516 from Bhutan in 2008.

In terms of resettlement *departures*, in 2008, 65,548 refugees were resettled in 26 countries, up from 49,868 in 2007. The largest number of UNHCR-assisted departures were from Thailand (16,807), Nepal (8,165), Syria (7,153), Jordan (6,704) and Malaysia (5,865). Note that these are the countries that refugees were resettled from, not their countries of origin.

A number of third countries run specific resettlement programmes in co-operation with UNHCR. The size of these programmes is shown in the table. The largest programmes are run by the United States, Canada and Australia. More than 2.4 million refugees resettled to the United States since 1980. A number of European countries run smaller schemes and in 2004 the United Kingdom established its own scheme, known as the Gateway Protection Programme with an initial quota of 500 (2004), which rose to 750 in the financial year 2009/10.

In September 2009, the European Commission unveiled plans for new Joint EU Resettlement Programme. The scheme would involve EU member states deciding together each year which refugees should be given priority. Member states would receive €4,000 from the European Refugee Fund per refugee resettled.

Between 1981, when Japan ratified the U.N. Convention Relating to the Status of Refugees, and 2002, Japan recognized only 305 persons as refugees. According to the UNHCR, in 2006 Japan accepted 26 refugees for resettlement.

### *Right of Return*

Even in a supposedly "post-conflict" environment, it is not a simple process for refugees to return home. The UN Pinheiro Principles are guided by the idea that not only people have the right to return home, but also to the same property. It seeks to return to the pre-conflict status quo and ensure that no one profits from the violence. Yet this is a very complex issue and every situation is different, conflict is a highly transformative force and the pre-war status-quo can never be reestablished completely, even if that were desirable (it may have caused the conflict n the first place). Therefore, the following are of particular importance to the right to return:

- may never have had property (e.g. in Afghanistan);
- cannot access what property they have (Colombia, Guatemala, South Africa and Sudan);
- ownership is unclear as families have expanded or split and division of the land becomes an issue;
- death of owner may leave dependents without clear claim to the land;
- people settled on the land know it is not theirs but have nowhere else to go (as in Colombia, Rwanda and Timor-Leste); and
- have completing claims with others, including the state and its foreign or local business partners (as in Aceh, Angola, Colombia, Liberia and Sudan).

## Law

Under international law, refugees are individuals who:

- are outside their country of nationality or habitual residence;
- have a well-founded fear of persecution because of their race, religion, nationality, membership in a particular social group or political opinion; and
- are unable or unwilling to avail themselves of the protection of that country, or to return there, for fear of persecution.

Refugee law encompasses both customary law, peremptory norms, and international legal instruments. These include:

- The 1951 United Nations Convention Relating to the Status of Refugees; also referred to as the Geneva Convention;
- The 1967 Protocol relating to the Status of Refugees;
- The 1969 OAU Convention Governing the Specific Aspects of Refugee Problems in Africa

## Historical and Contemporary Refugee Crises

### *Refugee Situations in the Middle East*

#### *Palestinian Refugees*

Following the 1948 proclamation of the State of Israel, the first Arab-Israeli War began. Many Palestinians had already left through their own choice, causing them to become refugees, and the Palestinian Exodus continued through the 1948 Arab-Israeli War and after the armistice that ended it. The great majority have remained refugees for generations as they were not permitted to settle in Israel or in the Arab countries where they lived. The refugee situation and the presence of numerous refugee camps continues to be a point of contention in the Arab-Israeli conflict. As of now they have not been accepted into any country for over 60 years.

The final estimate of refugee numbers was 711,000 according to the United Nations Conciliation Commission. Palestinian refugees from 1948 and their descendants do not come under the 1951 UN Convention Relating to the Status of Refugees, but under the UN Relief and Works Agency for Palestine Refugees in the Near East, which created its own criteria for refugee classification.

Palestine refugees are persons whose normal place of residence was Palestine between June 1946 and May 1948, who lost both their homes and means of livelihood as a result of the 1948 Arab-Israeli conflict. UNRWA's services are available to all those living in its area of operations who meet this definition, who are registered with the Agency and who need assistance. UNRWA's definition of a refugee also covers the descendants of persons who became refugees in 1948.

As such they are the only refugee population legally defined to include descendants of refugees, as well as others who might otherwise be considered internally displaced persons.

As of December 2005, the World Refugee Survey of the U.S. Committee for Refugees and Immigrants estimates the total number of Palestinian refugees and their descendants to be 2,966,100.

*Jewish Refugees*

Between the first and second world wars, Jewish immigration to Palestine was encouraged by the nascent Zionist movement but was restricted by the British Mandate government in Palestine. In Europe, Nazi persecution culminated in the Holocaust and the mass murder of many European Jews. The Evian Conference, Bermuda Conference, and others failed to resolve the problem of finding a home for large numbers of Jewish refugees from Nazi-occupied Europe. Following its formation in 1948, according to 1947 UN Partition Plan,Israel adopted the Law of Return, granting Israeli citizenship to any Jewish immigrant. Approximately 700,000 refugees flooded into the country, and were housed in tent cities called ma'abarot. After the dissolution of the USSR, a second surge of 700,000 Russian Jews fled to Israel between 1990 and 1995.

Jews have lived in what are now Arab states at least since the Babylonian captivity (597 BCE). The refusal of the Arab world to accept the existence of a Jewish state led to increased discrimination and violence against the Jews. In 1948, the Arab League declared the Jews enemy citizens. Jewish bank accounts and property was confiscated, Jews were arrested and fired from their jobs, and synagogues were attacked. In the early years after Israeli independence the number of Jews in Arab countries fell steeply: in Yemen, from 55,000 to 4,000; in Iraq from 135,000 to 6,000; in Aden from 8,000 to 800; in Egypt from 80,000 to 50,000; in Libya from 38,000 to 4,000; and in Syria from 30,000 to 5,000.

According to official Arab statistics, 856,000 Jews left their homes in Arab countries from 1948 until the early 1970s. Some 600,000 resettled in Israel. Their descendants, and those of Iranian and Turkish Jews, now number 3.06 million of Israel's 5.4 to 5.8 million Jewish citizens. The plight of the Jews in Arab lands worsened following the 1967 Six-Day War, prompting the exodus of most of the remaining Jewish population. Very few Jews live in Arab countries today.

In 2007, similar resolutions (H.Res.185 and S.Res.85) were proposed to the US Senate and Congress, to:

Make clear that the United States Government supports the position that, as an integral part of any comprehensive peace, the issue of refugees and the mass violations of human rights of minorities in Arab and Muslim countries throughout the Middle East, North Africa, and the Persian Gulf must be resolved in a manner that includes (A) consideration of the legitimate rights of all refugees displaced from Arab and Muslim countries throughout the Middle East, North Africa, and the Persian Gulf; and (B) recognition of the losses incurred by Jews, Christians, and other minority groups as a result of the Arab-Israeli conflict.

These resolutions were discussed on July 19, 2007 at the bicameral Congressional Human Rights Caucus in preparation for voting.

*African Refugees in Israel*

Since 2003, an estimated 10,000 non-Jewish immigrants from various African countries have crossed into Israel. Some 600 refugees from the Darfur region of Sudan have been granted temporary resident status to be renewed every year, though not official refugee state. Another 2,000 refugees from the conflict between Eritrea and Ethiopia have been granted temporary resident status on humanitarian grounds. Israel prefers not to recognize them as refugees so as not to offend Eritrea and Ethiopia. though Sudanese, who are from an enemy state, are also not recognized as refugees. In 2007, Israel deported 48 refugees back to Egypt after they succeeded in crossing the border, of which twenty were deported back to Sudan by Egyptian authorities, according to Amnesty International. In August 2008 the Israel Defense Forces deported at least another 91 African asylum seekers at the border. Throughout this year, Egyptian police have shot dead 20 African asylum seekers attempting to enter Israel. A Knesset bill entitled the "Anti-Infiltration Law" would allow the continuation of deportation back to Egypt within 72 hours.

*Refugees from the Algerian War*

The Algerian War of Independence (1954–1962) uprooted more than 2 million Algerians, who were forced to relocate in French camps or to flee to Morocco, Tunisia, and into the Algerian hinterland.

European-descended population, *Pieds-Noirs,* accounted for 10.4% of the total population of Algeria in 1962. In just a few months in 1962, 900,000 of them fled the country in the most massive relocation of population to Europe since the World War II. A motto used in the FLN propaganda designating the Pied-noirs community was "Suitcase or coffin" ("*La valise ou le cercueil*").

*Jordan*

Jordan has one of the world's largest immigrant population with some sources putting the immigrant percentage to being 60%. Jordan's religious toleration, political stability, and economic prosperity has made Jordan attractive to those fleeing violence and persecution. Jordan also has a higher quality of life compared to other countries in the region with high literacy rates, excellent healthcare infrastructure, and a relatively liberal social and economic environment. Palestinian refugees number almost half of Jordan's population, however they have assimilated into Jordanian society. Iraqi refugees number between 750,000 and 1 million with most living in Amman. Jordan also has Armenian, Chechen, and Circassian, and Mexican minorities

*Lebanon*

It is estimated that some 900,000 people, representing one-fifth of the pre-war population, were displaced from their homes during the Lebanese Civil War (1975–90).

The 2006 Lebanon War displaced approximately one million Lebanese and approximately 500,000 Israelis, although most were able to return to their homes. Lebanese desire to emigrate has increased since the war. Over a fifth of Shias, a quarter of Sunnis, and nearly half of Maronites have expressed the desire to leave Lebanon. Nearly a third of such Maronites have already submitted visa applications to foreign embassies, and another 60,000 Christians have already fled, as of April 2007. Lebanese Christians are concerned that their influence is waning, fear the apparent rise of radical Islam, and worry of potential Sunni-Shia rivalry.

*Western Sahara*

It is estimated that between 165,000 & 200,000 Sahrawis – people from the disputed territory of Western Sahara – have lived in five large refugee camps near Tindouf in the Algerian part of the Sahara Desert since 1975. The UNHCR and WFP are presently engaged in supporting what they describe as the "90,000 most vulnerable" refugees, giving no estimate for total refugee numbers.

*Nagorno Karabakh*

The Nagorno Karabakh conflict has resulted in the displacement of 528,000 (this figure does not include new born children of these IDPs) Azerbaijanis from Armenian occupied territories including Nagorno Karabakh, and 220,000 Azeris and 18,000 Kurds fled from Armenia to Azerbaijan from 1988 to 1989. 280,000 persons—virtually all ethnic Armenians—fled Azerbaijan during the 1988–1993 war over the disputed region of Nagorno-Karabakh. By the time both

Azerbaijan and Armenia had finally agreed to a ceasefire in 1994, an estimated 17,000 people had been killed, 50,000 had been injured, and over a million had been displaced.

*Turkey*

Between 1984 and 1999, the PKK and the Turkish military engaged in open war, and much of the countryside in the southeast was depopulated, with Kurdish civilians moving to local defensible centers such as Diyarbakýr, Van, and Þýrnak, as well as to the cities of western Turkey and even to western Europe. The causes of the depopulation included PKK atrocities against Kurdish clans they could not control, the poverty of the southeast, and the Turkish state's military operations. Human Rights Watch has documented many instances where the Turkish military forcibly evacuated villages, destroying houses and equipment to prevent the return of the inhabitants. An estimated 3,000 Kurdish villages in Turkey were virtually wiped from the map, representing the displacement of more than 378,000 people.

*Refugees from the Iraq Wars*

The Iran–Iraq War from 1980 to 1988, the 1990 Iraqi invasion of Kuwait, the first Gulf War and subsequent conflicts all generated hundreds of thousands if not millions of refugees. Iran also provided asylum for 1,400,000 Iraqi refugees who had been uprooted as a result of the Persian Gulf War (1990–91). At least one million Iraqi Kurds were displaced during the Al-Anfal Campaign (1986–1989).

The current Iraq war has generated millions of refugees and internally displaced persons. As of 2007 more Iraqis have lost their homes and become refugees than the population of any other country. Over 4,700,000 people, more than 16% of the Iraqi population, have become uprooted. Of these, about 2 million have fled Iraq and flooded other countries, and 2.7 million are estimated to be refugees inside Iraq, with nearly 100,000 Iraqis fleeing to Syria and Jordan each month. Only 1% of the total Iraqi displaced population was estimated to be in the Western countries.

Roughly 40% of Iraq's middle class is believed to have fled, the U.N. said. Most are fleeing systematic persecution and have no desire to return. All kinds of people, from university professors to bakers, have been targeted by militias, insurgents and criminals. An estimated 331 school teachers were slain in the first four months of 2006, according to Human Rights Watch, and at least 2,000 Iraqi doctors have been killed and 250 kidnapped since the 2003 U.S. invasion. Iraqi refugees in Syria and Jordan live in impoverished communities with little international attention to their plight and little legal protection. In Syria alone an estimated 50,000 Iraqi girls and women, many of them widows, are forced into prostitution just to survive.

According to Washington based Refugees International, out of the 4.2 million refugees fewer than 800 have been allowed into the US since the 2003 invasion. Sweden had accepted 18,000 and Australia had resettled almost 6,000. By 2006 Sweden had granted protection to more Iraqis than all the other EU Member States combined. However, and following repeated unanswered calls to its European partners for greater solidarity, July 2007 saw Sweden introduce a more restrictive policy towards Iraqi asylum seekers, which is expected to reduce the recognition rate in 2008.

As of September 2007 Syria had decided to implement a strict visa regime to limit the number of Iraqis entering the country at up to 5,000 per day, cutting the only accessible escape route for thousands of refugees fleeing the civil war in Iraq. A government decree that took effect on 10 September 2007 bars Iraqi passport holders from entering Syria except for businessmen and academics. Until then, the Syria was the only country that had resisted strict entry regulations for Iraqis.

*Religious Minorities in the Middle East*

Although Assyrian Christians represent less than 5% of the total Iraqi population, they make up 40% of the refugees fleeing Iraq, according to U.N. High Commissioner for Refugees. In the 16th century, Christians were half the population of Iraq. In 1987, the last Iraqi census counted 1.4 million Christians. But as the current war has radicalized Islamic sensibilities, Christians have seen their total numbers slump to about 500,000 today, of whom 250,000 live in Baghdad.

Furthermore, the small Mandaean and Yazidi communities are at the risk of elimination due to ethnic cleansing by Islamic militants. Entire neighborhoods in Baghdad were ethnically cleansed by Shia and Sunni Militias. Satellite shows ethnic cleansing in Iraq was key factor in "surge" success.

The US government position on refugees states that there is repression of religious minorities in the Middle East and in Pakistan such as Christians, Hindus, as well as Ahmadi, and Zikri denominations of Islam. In Sudan where Islam is the state religion, Muslims dominate the Government and restrict activities of Christians, practitioners of traditional African indigenous religions and other non-Muslims. The question of Jewish, Christian and other refugees from Arab and Muslim countries was introduced in March 2007 in the US congress.

In the Islamic republic of Iran, Iranian Christians decry minority religions' lack of freedom in Islamic countries, while Bahá'ís are also fleeing religious persecution.

### *Refugee Movements in Asia*

#### *Afghanistan*

From the Soviet invasion of Afghanistan in 1979 until the late 2001 US-led invasion, about six million Afghan refugees have fled to neighboring Pakistan (mainly NWFP) and Iran, making Afghanistan the largest refugee-producing country. Since early 2002, more than 5 million Afghan refugees have repatriated through the UNHCR from both Pakistan and Iran back to their native country, Afghanistan. Approximately 3.5 million from Pakistan while the remaining 1.5 million from Iran. Since 2007 the Iranian government has forcibly deported mostly unregistered (and some registered) Afghan refugees back to Afghanistan, with 362,000 being deported in 2008.

As of March 2009, some 1.7 million registered Afghan refugees still remain in Pakistan. This include the many who were born in Pakistan during the last 30 years but still counted as citizens of Afghanistan. They are allowed to work and study until the end of 2012. 935,600 registered Afghans are living in Iran, which also include the ones born inside Iran.

#### *Dissolution of the British Raj, the Partition of 1947 and Independence*

The partition of the British Raj provinces of Panjab and Bangal and the subsequent independence of Pakistan and one day later of India in 1947 resulted in the largest human movement in history. In this population exhange approximately 7 million Hindus and Sikhs from Bangladesh and Pakistan moved to India while approximately 7 million Muslims from India moved to Pakistan. Approximately one million Muslims, Hindus and Sikhs died during this event.

#### *Bangladeshi Refugees in India in 1971*

As a result of the Bangladesh Liberation War, on 27

March 1971, Prime Minister of India, Indira Gandhi, expressed full support of her Government to the Bangladeshi struggle for freedom. The Bangladesh-India border was opened to allow panic-stricken Bangladeshis' safe shelter in India. The governments of West Bengal, Bihar, Assam, Meghalaya and Tripura established refugee camps along the border. Exiled Bangladeshi army officers and the Indian military immediately started using these camps for recruitment and training members of Mukti Bahini. During the Bangladesh War of Independence around 10 million Bangladeshis fled the country to escape the killings and atrocities committed by the Pakistan Army. Bangladeshi refugees known as '"Chakmas"' in India.

*Pakistani Bihari Refugees in Bangladesh after 1971*

During the period of united Pakistan (1947-1971), the Urdu-speaking Biharis were not assimilated with in the society of East Pakistan and remained as a distinct cultural-linguistic group. Due to being of different linguistic group they were assaulted by Bengalis and Indian Army in 1971 war. Many atrocities took place against Biharis and even after war to date they are still living in the same conditions. At the end of war many Biharis took shelter in the refugee camps in different cities biggest being in Dhaka the Geneva Camp. It is estimated at about 250,000 biharis are living in worse conditions in those camp even today, with problems like continuous atrocities by Bengali local population, rape on young girls, malnutrition and poor hygiene and living conditions.

*Rohingya Refugees in Bangladesh and Pakistan from Burma*

Bangladesh hosts more than 250,000 Muslim Rohingya refugees forced from western Burma (Myanmar) who fled in 1991-92 to escape persecution by the Burmese military junta. Many have lived there for close to twenty years. The Bangladeshi government divides the Rohingya into two categories - recognized refugees living in official camps and unrecognized refugees living in unofficial sites or among Bangladeshi communities. Around 30,000 Rohingyas are residing in two camps in Nayapara and Kutupalong area of Cox's Bazar district in Bangladesh.

These camp residents have access to basic services, those outside do not. With no changes inside Burma in sight, Bangladesh must come to terms with the long-term needs of all the Rohingya refugees in the country, and allow international organizations to expand services that benefit the Rohingya as well as local communities. The agency has been supporting Rohingya refugees staying in the camps. On the other hand, it is not receiving applications for refugee status from the newly arrived Rohingyas. This amounts to compromising of its mandate. The brutal campaign of ethnic cleansing of Muslims in Arakan State by the Burmese military in 1991-92 thousands of people have been detained in crowded refugee camps in Bangladesh and tens of thousands have been repatriated to Burma to face further repression.

There are widespread allegations of religious persecution, use of forced labor and denial of citizenship of many Rohingya forced to return to Burma since 1996. Many have fled again to Bangladesh to seek work or shelter, or flee from Burmese military oppression, and some are forced across the border by Burmese security forces. In the past few months, abuses against Rohingya in Arakan State has continued, including strict registration laws that continue to deny Rohingya citizenship, restrictions on movement, land confiscation and forced evictions to make way for Buddhist Burmese settlements, widespread forced labor in infrastructure projects and closure of some mosques, including nine in North Buthidaung Township of Western Arakan State in the last half of 2006.

There are also large number of Muslim Rohingya refugees in Pakistan. Most of them have made perilous journey across Bangladesh and India and have settled in Karachi.

*The Himalayas*

After the 1959 Tibetan exodus, there are more than 150,000 Tibetans who live in India, many in settlements in Dharamsala and Mysore, and Nepal. These include people who have escaped over the Himalayas from Tibet, as well as their children and grandchildren. In India the overwhelming majority of Tibetans born in India are still stateless and carry a document called an Identity Card issued by the Indian government in lieu of a passport. This document states the nationality of the holder as Tibetan. It is a document that is frequently rejected as a valid travel document by many customs and immigrations departments. The Tibetan refugees also own a Green Book issued by the Tibetan Government in Exile for rights and duties towards this administration.

In 1991–92, Bhutan expelled roughly 100,000 ethnic Nepalis most of whom have been living in seven refugee camps in eastern Nepal ever since. In March 2008, this population began a multiyear resettlement to third countries including the United States, New Zealand, Denmark and Australia. At present, the United States is working towards resettling more than 60,000 of these refugees in the US as a third country settlement programme.

Meanwhile, as many as 200,000 Nepalese were displaced during the Maoist insurgency and Nepalese Civil War which ended in 2006.

More than 3 million Pakistani civilians have been displaced by War in North-West Pakistan (2004–Present) between the Pakistani government and Taliban militants.

*Sri Lankan Tamils*

The civil war in Sri Lanka (1983 to 2009) has generated millions of internally displaced as well as refugees. Sri Lanka Tamils have fled to India, Canada (over 103,625 people), and Europe (particularly France, Denmark, the United Kingdom, and Germany). Tamils prefer to come to Australia via Malaysia and Indonesia. Refugees travel through Malaysia and/or Thailand and Indonesia before moving into Australia or Canada by illegal means such as boat or plane. They pay between $10,000 and $20,000 USD to traffickers.

*Kashmir*

An estimated 1.5 to 2.6 million Kashmiri's have fled Indian-occupied Kashmir and now live in refugee camps in Pakistan's Azad Kashmir and several of its urban centres since the arrival and subsequent forcible occupation of the Kashmiri state by Indian troops. During 1980s and 1990s many Hindus were settled in the areas of Jammu by the Indian Government in order to make the proportion of Hindus in the valley more or equal to that of Muslims. Many displaced Muslims took shelter in Azad Kashmir in Pakistan. Some 100,000 Kashmiri Pandit Hindus (conservative estimate) have been internally displaced from Kashmr by separatist organizations seeking to liberate Kashmir from Indian rule. According to the National Human Rights Commission, about 300,000 Kashmiri Pandits have been forced to leave Kashmir. But Kashmiri groups peg the number of migrants closer to 500,000.

*Tajikistan Civil War*

Since 1991, much of the country's non-Muslim population, including Russians and Jews, have fled Tajikistan due to severe poverty, instability and Tajikistan Civil War (1992–1997). In 1992, most of the country's Jewish population was evacuated to Israel. By the end of the civil war Tajikistan was in a state of complete devastation. Around 1.2 million people were refugees inside and outside of the country.

*Uzbekistan*

In 1989, after bloody pogroms against the Meskhetian Turks in Central Asia's Ferghana Valley, nearly 90,000 Meskhetian Turks left Uzbekistan.

The 2010 South Kyrgyzstan riots left some 300,000 people internally displaced. Another 100,000 refugees crossed the border into Uzbekistan.

*Southeast Asia (Vietnam War)*

Following the communist takeovers in Vietnam, Cambodia, and Laos in 1975, about three million people attempted to escape in the subsequent decades. With massive influx of refugees daily, the resources of the receiving countries were severely strained. The plight of the boat people became an international humanitarian crisis. The United Nations High Commissioner for Refugees (UNHCR) set up refugee camps in neighboring countries to process the boat people. The budget of the UNHCR increased from $80 million in 1975 to $500 million in 1980. Partly for its work in Indochina, the UNHCR was awarded the 1981 Nobel Peace Prize.

- Large numbers of Vietnamese refugees came into existence after 1975 when South Vietnam fell to the communist forces. Many tried to escape, some by boat, thus giving rise to the phrase "boat people". The Vietnamese refugees emigrated to Hong Kong, France, the United States, Canada, Australia, and other countries, creating sizeable expatriate communities, notably in the United States. Since 1975, an estimated 1.4 million refugees from Vietnam and other Southeast Asian countries have been resettled to the United States. Most Asian countries were unwilling to accept refugees.

- Survivors of the Khmer Rouge regime in Cambodia fled across the border into Thailand after the Vietnamese invasion of 1978–79. Approximately 300,000 of these people were eventually resettled in the United States, France, Canada, and Australia between 1979 and 1992, when the camps were closed and the remaining people repatriated.
- Nearly 400,000 Laotians fled to Thailand after the Vietnam War and Communist Take over in 1975.Some left because of persecution by the government for religious or ethnic purposes.Most left between 1976–1985 and lived in refugee camps along the border between Thailand and Laos.They mostly settled in the United States, Canada, France , and Australia.In the United States they mostly settled in Washington State, California, Washington DC, Texas, Virginia, and Minnesota.
- The Mien or Yao recently lived in northern Vietnam, northern Laos and northern Thailand. In 1975, the Pathet Lao forces began seeking reprisal for the involvement of many Mien as soldiers in the CIA-sponsored Secret War in Laos. As a token of appreciation to the Mien and Hmong people who served in the CIA secret army, the United States accepted many of the refugees as naturalized citizens (Mien American). Many more Hmong continue to seek asylum in neighboring Thailand.
- Due to the persecution of the ethnic Karen, Karenni and other minority populations in Burma (Myanmar) significant numbers of refugees live along the Thai

border in camps of up to 100,000 people.

- Muslim ethnic groups from Burma, the Rohingya and other Arakanese have been living in camps in Bangladesh since the 1990s.

### *Refugees in Africa*

Since the 1950s, many nations in Africa have suffered civil wars and ethnic strife, thus generating a massive number of refugees of many different nationalities and ethnic groups. The division of Africa into European colonies in 1885, along which lines the newly independent nations of the 1950s and 1960s drew their borders, has been cited as a major reason why Africa has been so plagued with intrastate warfare. The number of refugees in Africa increased from 860,000 in 1968 to 6,775,000 by 1992. By the end of 2004, that number had dropped to 2,748,400 refugees, according to the United Nations High Commission for Refugees. (That figure does not include internally displaced persons, who do not cross international borders and so do not fit the official definition of refugee.)

Many refugees in Africa cross into neighboring countries to find haven; often, African countries are simultaneously countries of origin for refugees and countries of asylum for other refugees. The Democratic Republic of Congo, for instance, was the country of origin for 462,203 refugees at the end of 2004, but a country of asylum for 199,323 other refugees.

Countries in Africa from where 5,000 or more refugees originated as of the end of 2004, arranged in descending order of numbers of refugees are listed below. The largest number of refugees are from Sudan and have fled either the longstanding and recently concluded Sudanese Civil War or the Darfur conflict and are located mainly in Chad, Uganda, Ethiopia, and Kenya.

- Angola: 228,838
- Burundi: 485,764
- Cameroon: 7,629
- Central African Republic: 31,069
- Chad: 52,663
- Côte d'Ivoire: 23,655
- Democratic Republic of Congo: 462,203
- Eritrea: 131,119
- Ethiopia: 63,105
- Ghana: 14,767
- Liberia: 335,467
- Nigeria: 23,888
- Republic of the Congo: 28,152
- Rwanda: 63,808
- Senegal: 8,332
- Sierra Leone: 41,801
- Somalia: 389,272
- Sudan: 930,612
- Togo: 10,819
- Uganda: 31,963
- Zimbabwe: 9,568

*Angola*

Decolonisation during the 1960s and 1970s often resulted in the mass exodus of European-descended settlers out of Africa – especially from North Africa (1.6 million European *pieds noirs*), Congo, Mozambique and Angola. By the mid-1970s, the Portugal's African territories were lost, and nearly one million Portuguese or persons of Portuguese descent left those territories (mostly Portuguese Angola and Mozambique) as destitute refugees – the *retornados*.

The Angolan Civil War (1975–2002), one of the largest and deadliest Cold War conflicts, erupted shortly after and spread out across the newly-independent country. At least one million persons were killed, four million were displaced internally and another half million fled as refugees.

*Uganda*

In the 1970s Uganda and other East African nations implemented racist policies that targeted the Asian population of the region. Uganda under Idi Amin's leadership was particularly most virulent in its anti-Asian policies, eventually resulting in the expulsion and ethnic cleansing of Uganda's Asian minority. Uganda's 80,000 Asians were mostly Indians born in the country. India had refused to accept them. Most of the expelled Indians eventually settled in the United Kingdom, Canada and in the United States.

*Great Lakes Refugee Crisis*

In the aftermath of the 1994 Rwandan Genocide, over two million people fled into neighboring countries, in particular Zaire. The refugee camps were soon controlled by the former government and Hutu militants who used the camps as bases to launch attacks against the new government in Rwanda. Little action was taken to resolve the situation and the crisis did not end until Rwanda-supported rebels forced the refugees back across the border at the beginning of the First Congo War.

*Darfur*

An estimated 2.5 million people, roughly one-third the population of the Darfur area, have been forced to flee their homes after attacks by Janjaweed Arab militia backed by

Sudanese troops during the ongoing Darfur conflict in western Sudan since roughly 2003.

### *Refugee Movements in and Within Europe*

#### *European Union*

The European Union is developing a common system for immigration and asylum and a single external border control strategy. This involves categorising refugees as separate from economic migrants – i.e. as political migrants which includes the categories illegal immigrants, asylum seekers, and as refugees.

According to the European Council on Refugees and Exiles, a network of European refugee-assisting non-governmental organizations (NGOs), huge differences exist between national asylum systems in Europe, making the asylum system a 'lottery' for refugees. For example, Iraqis who flee their home country and end up in Germany have a 85% of being recognised as a refugee and those who apply for asylum in Slovenia do not get a protection status at all. A phenomenon referred to as 'secondary movement' describes the travelling of asylum seekers from one country of the European Union to another.

In France, helping an illegal immigrant (providing shelter, for example) is prohibited by a law passed on December 27, 1994. The law was heavily criticized by (NGOs) such as the CIMADE and the GISTI, left-wing political parties such as the Greens and the Communists, and trade unions such as the magistrates' *Syndicat de la magistrature*.

The Turkish newspaper *Hürriyet* published stories in July 2004 and May 2006 that Hellenic Coast Guard ships were caught on film cruising as near as a few hundred meters off the Turkish coast and abandoning clandestine immigrants to the sea. This practice allegedly resulted in the drowning of six people between Chios and Karaburun Peninsula on 26 September 2006 while three others disappeared and 31 were saved by Turkish gendarmes and fishermen.

A tough new EU immigration law detaining illegal immigrants for up to 18 months before deportation has triggered outrage across Latin America, with Venezuelan President Hugo Chavez threatening to cut off oil exports to Europe.

*Hungary*

In 1956–57 following the Hungarian Revolution of 1956 nearly 200,000 persons, about two percent of the population of Hungary, fled as refugees to Austria and West Germany.

*Czechoslovakia*

The Warsaw Pact invasion of Czechoslovakia in 1968 was followed by a wave of emigration, unseen before and stopped shortly after (estimate: 70,000 immediately, 300,000 in total), typic

*Cyprus*

It is estimated that 40% of the Greek population of Cyprus, as well as over half of the Turkish Cypriot population, were displaced by the Turkish invasion of Cyprus in 1974. The figures for internally displaced Cypriots varies, the United Peacekeeping force in Cyprus (UNFICYP) estimates 165,000 Greek Cypriots and 45,000 Turkish Cypriots. The UNHCR registers slightly higher figures of 200,000 and 65,000 respectively, being partly based on official Cypriot statistics which register children of displaced families as refugees. The separation of the two communities via the UN patrolled Green Line prohibited the return of all internally displaced people.

*Balkans*

Following the Greek Civil War (1946–1949) hundreds of thousands of Greeks and Ethnic Macedonians were expelled or fled the country. The number of refugees ranged from 35,000 to over 213,000. Over 28,000 children were evacuated by the Partisans to the Eastern Bloc and the Socialist Republic of Macedonia. This left thousands of Greeks and Aegean Macedonians spread across the world.

The forced assimilation campaign of the late 1980s directed against ethnic Turks resulted in the emigration of some 300,000 Bulgarian Turks to Turkey. Beginning in 1991, political upheavals in the Balkans such as the breakup of Yugoslavia, displaced about 2,700,000 people by mid-1992, of which over 700,000 of them sought asylum in Europe. In 1999, about one million Albanians escaped from Serbian persecution.

Today there are still thousands of refugees and internally displaced persons in the Balkan Region who cannot return to their homes. Most of them are Serbs who cannot return to Kosovo, and who still live in refugee camps in Serbia today. Over 200,000 Serbs and other non-Albanian minorities fled or were expelled from Kosovo after the Kosovo War in 1999.

Refugees and IDPs in Serbia form between 7% and 7.5% of its population – about half a million refugees sought refuge in the country following the series of Yugoslav wars (from Croatia mainly, to an extent Bosnia and Herzegovina too and the IDPs from Kosovo, which are the most numerous at over 200,000). Serbia has the largest refugee population in Europe.

*Chechnya*

From 1992 ongoing conflict has taken place in Chechenya,

Caucasus due to independence proclaimed by this republic in 1991 which is not accepted by the Russian Federation or any other state in the world. As a consequence about 2 million people have been displaced and still cannot return to their homes. At the end of the Soviet era, ethnic Russians comprised about 23% of the population (269,000 in 1989). Due to widespread lawlessness and ethnic cleansing under the government of Dzhokhar Dudayev most non-Chechens (and many Chechens as well) fled the country during the 1990s or were killed.

*Georgia*

More than 250,000 people, mostly Georgians but some others too, were the victims of forcible displacement and ethnic-cleansing from Abkhazia during the War in Abkhazia between 1992 and 1993, and afterwards in 1993 and 1998.

As a result of 1991–1992 South Ossetia War, about 100,000 ethnic Ossetians fled South Ossetia and Georgia proper, most across the border into North Ossetia. A further 23,000 ethnic Georgians fled South Ossetia and settled in other parts of Georgia.

The United Nations estimated 100,000 Georgians have been uprooted as a result of the 2008 South Ossetia war; some 30,000 residents of South Ossetia fled into the neighboring Russian province of North Ossetia.

***Movements in the Americas***

*Displaced Latin Americans*

More than one million Salvadorans were displaced during the Salvadoran Civil War from 1975 to 1982. About half went to the United States, most settling in the Los Angeles area. There was also a large exodus of Guatemalans during the 1980s, trying to escape from the Civil War and genocide there as well. These people went to Southern Mexico and the U.S.

From 1991 through 1994, following the military coup d'état against President Jean-Bertrand Aristide, thousands of Haitians fled violence and repression by boat. Although most were repatriated to Haiti by the U.S. government, others entered the United States as refugees. Haitians were primarily regarded as economic migrants from the grinding poverty of Haiti, the poorest nation in the Western Hemisphere.

The victory of the forces led by Fidel Castro in the Cuban Revolution led to a large exodus of Cubans between 1959 and 1980. Dozens of Cubans yearly continue to risk the waters of the Straits of Florida seeking better economic and political conditions in the U.S. In 1999 the highly publicized case of six year old Elián González brought the covert migration to international attention. Measures by both governments have attempted to address the issue; the U.S. instituted a wet feet, dry feet policy allowing refuge to those travelers who manage to complete their journey, and the Cuban government have periodically allowed for mass migration by organizing leaving posts. The most famous of these agreed migrations was the Mariel boatlift of 1980.

Colombia has one of the world's largest populations of internally displaced persons (IDPs), with estimates ranging from 2.6 to 4.3 million people, due to the ongoing Colombian armed conflict. The larger figure is cumulative since 1985. It is now estimated by the U.S. Committee for Refugees and Immigrants that there are about 150,000 Colombians in "refugee-like situations" in the United States, not recognized as refugees or subject to any formal protection.

*United States*

During the Vietnam War, many U.S. citizens who were

conscientious objectors and wished to avoid the draft sought political asylum in Canada. President Jimmy Carter issued an amnesty. Since 1975, the U.S. has resettled approximately 2.6 million refugees, with nearly 77% being either Indochinese or citizens of the former Soviet Union. Since the enactment of the Refugee Act of 1980, annual admissions figures have ranged from a high of 207,116 in 1980 to a low of 27,100 in 2002.

Currently, ten national voluntary agencies resettle refugees nationwide on behalf of the U.S. government: Church World Service, Ethiopian Community Development Council, Episcopal Migration Ministries, Hebrew Immigrant Aid Society, International Rescue Committee, U.S. Committee for Refugees and Immigrants, Lutheran Immigration and Refugee Service, United States Conference of Catholic Bishops, World Relief and State of Iowa, Bureau of Refugee Services.

The U.S. Office of Refugee Resettlement (ORR) funds a number of organizations that provide technical assistance to voluntary agencies and local refugee resettlement organizations. RefugeeWorks, headquartered in Baltimore, Maryland, is ORR's training and technical assistance arm for employment and self-sufficiency activities, for example. This nonprofit organization assists refugee service providers in their efforts to help refugees achieve self-sufficiency. RefugeeWorks publishes white papers, newsletters and reports on refugee employment topics.

### *Unaccompanied Refugee Minors in the United States*

An Unaccompanied Refugee Minor (URM) is any person who has not attained 18 years of age who entered the United States unaccompanied by and not destined to: (a) a parent, or (b) a close non-parental adult relative who is willing and able to care for said minor, or (c) an adult with a clear and court-verifiable claim to custody of the minor; and who has no parent(s) in the United States. Trafficking victims who have been certified by the U.S. Department of Health and Human Services, are also eligible for benefits and services under this program, to the same extent as refugees.

The URM program is coordinated by the U.S. Office of Refugee Resettlement (ORR), a branch of the United States Administration for Children and Families. The mission of the ORR is to provide people in need with critical resources to assist them in becoming integrated members of American society.

ORR contracts with two faith-based agencies to manage the URM program in the United States; Lutheran Immigration and Refugee Service (LIRS) and the United States Conference of Catholic Bishops (USCCB). These agencies identify eligible children in need of URM services; determine appropriate placements for children among their national networks of affiliated agencies; and conduct training, research and technical assistance on URM services. They also provide the social services such as: indirect financial support for housing, food, clothing, medical care and other necessities; intensive case management by social workers; independent living skills training; educational supports; English language training; career/college counseling and training; mental health services; assistance adjusting immigration status; cultural activities; recreational opportunities; support for social integration; and cultural and religious preservation.

The URM services provided through these contracts are not available in all areas of the United States. The 14 states that participate in the URM program include: Arizona, California, Colorado, Florida, Massachusetts, Michigan, Mississippi, North Dakota, New York, Pennsylvania, Texas,

Utah, Virginia, Washington and the nation's capital, Washington D.C.

Although they are in the United States without the protection of their family, URM-designated children are not generally eligible for adoption. This is due in part to the Hague Convention on the Protection and Co-Operation in Respect of Inter-Country Adoption, otherwise known as the Hague Convention. Created in 1993, the Hague Convention established international standards for inter-country adoption. In order to protect against the abduction, sale or trafficking of children, these standards protect the rights of the biological parents of all children. Children in the URM program have become separated from their biological parents and the ability to find and gain parental release of URM children is often extremely difficult. Most children, therefore, are not adopted. They are served primarily through the foster care system of the participating states. Most will be in the custody of the state (typically living with a foster family) until they become adults. Reunification with the child's family is encouraged whenever possible.

Perhaps the most commonly known group to enter the United States through the URM program was known as the "Lost Boys" of Sudan. Their story was made into a documentary by Megan Mylan and Jon Shenk. The film, Lost Boys of Sudan, follows two Sudanese refugees on their journey from Africa to America. It won an Independent Spirit Award and earned two national Emmy nominations.

According to the Administration for Children and Families, as of 2009, there were 700 Unaccompanied Refugee Minors in the United States. Since its inception in the 1980s over 13,000 children have been served through this program.

# Appendix

## REFUGEE POPULATION IN THE WORLD

| *Rank* | *Country / Territory* | *Total Population* | *Refugee Population* | *Natives per Refugee* |
|---|---|---|---|---|
| – | **World** | **6,865,100,000** | **13,599,900** | **505** |
| 1 | *Palestine* | 3,761,646 | 1,828,100 | 2 |
| 2 | Jordan | 6,316,000 | 621,600 | 10 |
| 3 | Syria | 21,906,000 | 1,763,900 | 12 |
| 4 | Lebanon | 4,224,000 | 333,500 | 13 |
| 5 | Chad | 11,206,000 | 330,500 | 34 |
| 6 | Iran | 74,196,000 | 993,600 | 75 |
| 7 | Kuwait | 2,985,000 | 40,000 | 75 |
| 8 | Cyprus | 801,600 | 10,000 | 80 |
| 9 | Botswana | 1,950,000 | 23,100 | 84 |
| 10 | Saudi Arabia | 25,721,000 | 291,100 | 88 |
| 11 | Republic of the Congo | 3,683,000 | 40,000 | 92 |
| 12 | Pakistan | 170,387,500 | 1,775,600 | 96 |
| 13 | Djibouti | 864,000 | 8,800 | 98 |
| 14 | Ecuador | 14,036,775 | 135,000 | 104 |
| 15 | Kenya | 39,802,000 | 377,400 | 105 |
| 16 | Mauritania | 3,291,000 | 30,600 | 108 |
| 17 | Gabon | 1,475,000 | 13,100 | 113 |
| 18 | Gambia | 1,705,000 | 14,900 | 114 |
| 19 | Venezuela | 28,456,383 | 211,000 | 135 |
| 20 | Tanzania | 43,739,000 | 321,900 | 136 |
| 21 | Zambia | 12,935,000 | 88,900 | 146 |
| 22 | Serbia | 9,850,000 | 66,600 | 148 |
| 23 | Malaysia | 27,468,000 | 171,500 | 160 |

| | | | | |
|---|---|---|---|---|
| 24 | Yemen | 23,580,000 | 145,700 | 162 |
| 25 | Rwanda | 9,998,000 | 59,000 | 169 |
| 26 | Thailand | 63,389,730 | 368,800 | 172 |
| 27 | Sudan | 42,272,000 | 233,900 | 181 |
| 28 | Namibia | 2,171,000 | 11,700 | 186 |
| 29 | South Africa | 49,320,000 | 256,200 | 193 |
| 30 | Guinea-Bissau | 1,611,000 | 8,300 | 194 |
| 31 | Panama | 3,454,000 | 17,200 | 201 |
| 32 | Uganda | 32,710,000 | 155,400 | 210 |
| 33 | Cameroon | 19,522,000 | 91,900 | 212 |
| 34 | Nepal | 29,331,000 | 121,300 | 242 |
| 35 | Costa Rica | 4,579,000 | 18,600 | 246 |
| 36 | Burundi | 8,303,000 | 26,300 | 316 |
| 37 | Greece | 11,257,285 | 34,300 | 328 |
| 38 | Sierra Leone | 5,696,000 | 17,200 | 331 |
| 39 | Libya | 6,420,000 | 18,900 | 340 |
| 40 | Dem. Rep. of Congo | 66,020,000 | 192,700 | 343 |
| 41 | Senegal | 12,534,000 | 35,900 | 349 |
| 42 | Guinea | 10,069,000 | 28,100 | 358 |
| 43 | Algeria | 34,895,000 | 96,500 | 362 |
| 44 | Norway | 4,834,000 | 13,300 | 363 |
| 45 | Sweden | 9,292,359 | 23,400 | 397 |
| 46 | Israel | 7,434,000 | 16,500 | 451 |
| 48 | Central African Republic | 4,422,000 | 9,100 | 486 |
| 49 | Egypt | 77,116,112 | 152,400 | 506 |
| 50 | Bosnia and Herzegovina | 3,767,000 | 7,400 | 509 |
| 51 | Switzerland | 7,739,100 | 13,700 | 565 |
| 52 | Ethiopia | 79,221,000 | 135,200 | 586 |
| 53 | Somalia | 9,133,000 | 15,300 | 597 |
| 54 | Republic of Macedonia | 2,048,620 | 3,200 | 640 |
| 55 | Papua New Guinea | 6,732,000 | 10,000 | 673 |
| 56 | Austria | 8,355,260 | 12,200 | 685 |
| 57 | Armenia | 3,230,100 | 4,500 | 718 |
| 58 | Iraq | 30,747,000 | 39,500 | 778 |
| 59 | Côte d'Ivoire | 21,075,000 | 26,300 | 801 |
| 60 | Spain | 45,929,476 | 5,600 | 820 |

| | | | | |
|---|---|---|---|---|
| 61 | Bangladesh | 162,221,000 | 193,100 | 840 |
| 62 | Togo | 6,619,000 | 6,900 | 959 |
| 63 | Niger | 15,290,000 | 15,700 | 974 |
| 64 | Eritrea | 5,073,000 | 5,000 | 1015 |
| 65 | Benin | 8,935,000 | 8,400 | 1064 |
| 66 | Liberia | 3,476,608 | 18,800 | 1064 |
| 67 | Angola | 18,498,000 | 15,900 | 1163 |
| 68 | Mali | 13,010,000 | 11,100 | 1172 |
| 70 | Finland | 5,343,608 | 4,200 | 1272 |
| 71 | Ghana | 23,837,000 | 18,700 | 1275 |
| 72 | Malawi | 15,263,000 | 11,600 | 1316 |
| 73 | Russia | 141,803,000 | 107,000 | 1325 |
| 74 | Netherlands | 16,535,207 | 11,800 | 1401 |
| 75 | Germany | 82,046,000 | 54,200 | 1514 |
| 76 | Belgium | 10,754,528 | 7,100 | 1515 |
| 77 | Croatia | 4,435,056 | 2,600 | 1706 |
| 78 | Mozambique | 22,894,000 | 12,900 | 1775 |
| 79 | United States | 310,101,000 | 161,200 | 1924 |
| 80 | Denmark | 5,519,441 | 2,800 | 1971 |
| 81 | Australia | 22,268,000 | 9,900 | 2249 |
| 82 | United Kingdom | 61,634,599 | 26,600 | 2317 |
| 83 | India | 1,183,610,000 | 411,000 | 2880 |
| 84 | France | 65,073,482 | 22,300 | 2918 |
| 85 | Azerbaijan | 8,629,900 | 2,800 | 3082 |
| 86 | Italy | 60,088,880 | 19,000 | 3163 |
| 87 | Zimbabwe | 12,523,000 | 3,900 | 3211 |
| 88 | Czech Republic | 10,467,542 | 3,200 | 3271 |
| 89 | Kazakhstan | 15,776,492 | 4,500 | 3506 |
| 90 | Turkey | 71,517,100 | 18,200 | 3930 |
| 91 | People's Republic of China | 1,339,450,000 | 332,000 | 4034 |
| 92 | Poland | 38,100,700 | 5,700 | 6684 |
| 93 | Brazil | 193,539,000 | 21,400 | 9044 |
| 94 | Vietnam | 85,789,573 | 9,500 | 9030 |
| 95 | Nigeria | 154,729,000 | 9,200 | 16818 |
| 96 | South Korea | 48,333,000 | 2,500 | 19333 |

| | | | | |
|---|---|---|---|---|
| 97 | Mexico | 107,550,697 | 3,600 | 29875 |
| 98 | Japan | 127,590,000 | 3,100 | 41158 |
| 99 | Indonesia | 229,965,000 | unknown | unknown |
| 100 | Philippines | 92,222,660 | unknown | unknown |
| 101 | Myanmar (Burma) | 50,020,000 | unknown | unknown |
| 102 | Ukraine | 46,029,281 | unknown | unknown |
| 103 | Colombia | 45,064,807 | unknown | unknown |
| 104 | Argentina | 40,134,425 | unknown | unknown |
| 105 | Morocco | 31,567,613 | unknown | unknown |
| 106 | Peru | 29,132,013 | unknown | unknown |
| 107 | Afghanistan | 28,150,000 | unknown | unknown |
| 108 | Uzbekistan | 27,488,000 | unknown | unknown |
| 109 | North Korea | 24,051,706 | unknown | unknown |
| 110 | Taiwan | 23,069,345 | unknown | unknown |
| 111 | Romania | 21,498,616 | unknown | unknown |
| 112 | Sri Lanka | 20,238,000 | unknown | unknown |
| 113 | Madagascar | 19,625,000 | unknown | unknown |
| 114 | Chile | 17,121,000 | unknown | unknown |
| 115 | Burkina Faso | 15,757,000 | unknown | unknown |
| 116 | Cambodia | 14,805,000 | unknown | unknown |
| 117 | Guatemala | 14,027,000 | unknown | unknown |
| 118 | Cuba | 11,204,000 | unknown | unknown |
| 119 | Portugal | 10,627,250 | unknown | unknown |
| 120 | Tunisia | 10,327,800 | unknown | unknown |
| 121 | Dominican Republic | 10,090,000 | unknown | unknown |
| 122 | Haiti | 10,033,000 | unknown | unknown |
| 123 | Hungary | 10,031,208 | unknown | unknown |
| 124 | Bolivia | 9,863,000 | unknown | unknown |
| 125 | Belarus | 9,671,900 | unknown | unknown |
| 126 | Bulgaria | 7,606,551 | unknown | unknown |
| 127 | Honduras | 7,466,000 | unknown | unknown |
| 128 | *Hong Kong* | 7,008,900 | unknown | unknown |
| 129 | Tajikistan | 6,952,000 | unknown | unknown |
| 130 | Paraguay | 6,349,000 | unknown | unknown |
| 131 | Laos | 6,320,000 | unknown | unknown |
| 132 | El Salvador | 6,163,000 | unknown | unknown |

| | | | | |
|---|---|---|---|---|
| 133 | Nicaragua | 5,743,000 | unknown | unknown |
| 134 | Kyrgyzstan | 5,482,000 | unknown | unknown |
| 135 | Slovakia | 5,413,548 | unknown | unknown |
| 136 | Turkmenistan | 5,110,000 | unknown | unknown |
| 137 | Singapore | 4,839,400 | unknown | unknown |
| 138 | United Arab Emirates | 4,599,000 | unknown | unknown |
| 139 | Ireland | 4,422,100 | unknown | unknown |
| 140 | Georgia | 4,385,400 | unknown | unknown |
| 141 | New Zealand | 4,365,000 | unknown | unknown |
| 142 | *Puerto Rico* | 3,982,000 | unknown | unknown |
| 143 | Moldova | 3,567,500 | unknown | unknown |
| 144 | Uruguay | 3,361,000 | unknown | unknown |
| 145 | Lithuania | 3,349,872 | unknown | unknown |
| 146 | Albania | 3,170,000 | unknown | unknown |
| 147 | Oman | 2,845,000 | unknown | unknown |
| 148 | Jamaica | 2,719,000 | unknown | unknown |
| 149 | Mongolia | 2,671,000 | unknown | unknown |
| 150 | Latvia | 2,257,300 | unknown | unknown |
| 151 | Lesotho | 2,067,000 | unknown | unknown |
| 152 | Slovenia | 2,045,249 | unknown | unknown |
| 153 | Qatar | 1,409,000 | unknown | unknown |
| 154 | Estonia | 1,340,415 | unknown | unknown |
| 155 | Trinidad and Tobago | 1,339,000 | unknown | unknown |
| 156 | Mauritius | 1,288,000 | unknown | unknown |
| 157 | Swaziland | 1,185,000 | unknown | unknown |
| 158 | East Timor | 1,134,000 | unknown | unknown |
| 159 | Fiji | 849,000 | unknown | unknown |
| 160 | Bahrain | 791,000 | unknown | unknown |
| 161 | Guyana | 762,000 | unknown | unknown |
| 162 | Bhutan | 697,000 | unknown | unknown |
| 163 | Comoros | 676,000 | unknown | unknown |
| 164 | Equatorial Guinea | 676,000 | unknown | unknown |
| 165 | Montenegro | 624,000 | unknown | unknown |
| 166 | *Macau* | 546,200 | unknown | unknown |
| 167 | Solomon Islands | 523,000 | unknown | unknown |
| 168 | Suriname | 520,000 | unknown | unknown |

| | | | | |
|---|---|---|---|---|
| 169 | *Western Sahara* | 513,000 | unknown | unknown |
| 170 | Cape Verde | 506,000 | unknown | unknown |
| 171 | Luxembourg | 493,500 | unknown | unknown |
| 172 | Malta | 413,627 | unknown | unknown |
| 173 | Brunei | 400,000 | unknown | unknown |
| 174 | Bahamas | 342,000 | unknown | unknown |
| 175 | Belize | 322,100 | unknown | unknown |
| 176 | Iceland | 319,246 | unknown | unknown |
| 177 | Maldives | 309,000 | unknown | unknown |
| 178 | Barbados | 256,000 | unknown | unknown |
| 179 | Vanuatu | 240,000 | unknown | unknown |
| 180 | *Netherlands Antilles* | 198,000 | unknown | unknown |
| 181 | Samoa | 179,000 | unknown | unknown |
| 182 | *Guam* | 178,000 | unknown | unknown |
| 183 | Saint Lucia | 172,000 | unknown | unknown |
| 184 | São Tomé and Príncipe | 163,000 | unknown | unknown |
| 185 | Federated States of Micronesia | 111,000 | unknown | unknown |
| 186 | *U.S. Virgin Islands* | 110,000 | unknown | unknown |
| 187 | Saint Vincent and the Grenadines | 109,000 | unknown | unknown |
| 188 | *Aruba* | 107,000 | unknown | unknown |
| 189 | Grenada | 104,000 | unknown | unknown |
| 190 | Tonga | 104,000 | unknown | unknown |
| 191 | Kiribati | 98,000 | unknown | unknown |
| 192 | *Jersey* | 89,300 | unknown | unknown |
| 193 | Antigua and Barbuda | 88,000 | unknown | unknown |
| 194 | *Northern Mariana Islands* | 87,000 | unknown | unknown |
| 195 | Andorra | 86,000 | unknown | unknown |
| 196 | Seychelles | 84,000 | unknown | unknown |
| 197 | *Isle of Man* | 80,000 | unknown | unknown |
| 198 | Dominica | 67,000 | unknown | unknown |
| 199 | *American Samoa* | 67,000 | unknown | unknown |
| 200 | *Bermuda* | 65,000 | unknown | unknown |
| 201 | Marshall Islands | 62,000 | unknown | unknown |
| 202 | *Guernsey* | 61,811 | unknown | unknown |

| | | | | |
|---|---|---|---|---|
| 203 | *Greenland* | 57,000 | unknown | unknown |
| 204 | *Cayman Islands* | 56,000 | unknown | unknown |
| 205 | Saint Kitts and Nevis | 52,000 | unknown | unknown |
| 206 | *Faroe Islands* | 48,940 | unknown | unknown |
| 207 | Liechtenstein | 35,593 | unknown | unknown |
| 208 | Monaco | 33,000 | unknown | unknown |
| 209 | *Turks and Caicos Islands* | 33,000 | unknown | unknown |
| 210 | *Gibraltar* | 31,000 | unknown | unknown |
| 211 | San Marino | 30,800 | unknown | unknown |
| 212 | *British Virgin Islands* | 23,000 | unknown | unknown |
| 213 | *Cook Islands* | 20,000 | unknown | unknown |
| 214 | Palau | 20,000 | unknown | unknown |
| 215 | *Anguilla* | 15,000 | unknown | unknown |
| 216 | Tuvalu | 10,000 | unknown | unknown |
| 217 | Nauru | 10,000 | unknown | unknown |
| 218 | *Saint Helena* | 6,600 | unknown | unknown |
| 219 | *Montserrat* | 5,900 | unknown | unknown |
| 220 | *Falkland Islands* | 3,000 | unknown | unknown |
| 221 | *Niue* | 1,500 | unknown | unknown |
| 222 | *Tokelau* | 1,400 | unknown | unknown |
| 223 | Vatican City | 800 | unknown | unknown |
| 224 | *Pitcairn Islands* | 50 | unknown | unknown |

*Source:* http://en.wikipedia.org/wiki/List _of _countries_ by_ refugee_ Population.

# Bibliography

Allen, T. and H. Morsink, eds. (1994) *When Refugees Go Home.* London; James Currey.

Amnesty International (1997) *Refugees: Human Rights Have No Borders.* New York: Amnesty International Publications.

Bayefsky, Anne F. And Joan Fitzpatrick, eds. (2000) *Human Rights and Forced Displacement.* The Hague, Boston, and London: Martinus Nijhoff Publishers.

Bertrand, Maurice and Daniel Warner, eds. (1997) *A New Charter for a Worldwide Organization*? Dordrecht: Martinus Nijhoff.

Black, Richard (1998) *Refugees, Environment, and Development.* Essex, United Kingdom: Addison Wesley Longman Ltd.

Cernea, Michael Internal Refugee Flows and Development-Induced Population Displacement. *Journal of Refugee Studies* 3(4):320-339.

Cernea, Michael M. (1988) *Involuntary Resettlement in Development Projects: Policy Guidelines in World Bank-Financed Projects.* World Bank Technical Paper Number 80. Washington, D.C.: World Bank.

Cernea, Michael M. (1991) Involuntary Resettlement: Social Research, Policy, and Planning. In *Putting People First: Sociological Variables in Rural Development* (Second Edition). Michael M. Cernea, ed. pp. 188-215. New York: Oxford University Press.

Cernea, Michael M. (1995) Understanding and Preventing

Impoverishment from Displacement: Reflections from the State of Knowledge. *Journal of Refugee Studies* 8(3):245-264.

Cernea, Michael M. (1997) The Risks and Reconstruction Model for Resettling Displaced Populations. World Development 25(10):1569-1587.

Cernea, Michael M., ed. (1999) *The Economics of Involuntary Resettlement: Questions and Challenges.* Washington, D.C.: The World Bank.

Cernea, Michael M. and Scott E. Guggenheim, eds. (1993) *Anthropological Approaches to Resettlement: Policy, Practice, and Theory.* Boulder, Colorado: Westview Press.

Chambers, Robert (1969) *Settlement Schemes in Tropical Africa.* New York, New York: Praeger.

Chambers, Robert, ed. (1970) *The Social Consequences of Resettlement.* London: Pall Mall Press.

Chambers, Robert (1986) Hidden Losers? The Impact of Rural Refugees and Refugee Programs on Poorer Hosts. *International Migration Review* 20:245-265.

Clark, Sam, Elizabeth Colson, James Lee, and Thayer Scudder (1995) Ten Thousand Tonga: A Longitudinal Anthropological Study from Southern Zambia, 1956-1991. *Population Studies* 49(1):91-109.

Cohen, Roberta and Francis M., eds. (1998) *The Forsaken People: Case Studies of the Internally Displaced.* Washington, D.C.: Brookings Institution Press.

Colson, Elizabeth (1971) *The Social Consequences of Resettlement: The Impact of the Kariba Resettlement Experience Upon the Gwembe Tonga.* New York and Oxford: Oxford University Press.

Cook, Cynthia, ed. (1994) *Involuntary Resettlement in Development*

*Projects: Selected Papers fro, a Conference on Environment and Settlement Issues in Africa.* World Bank Technical Paper No. 237. Washington, D.C.: The World Bank.

Cuny, F., B. Stein, and P. Reed, eds. (1992) *Repatriation During Conflict in Africa and Asia.* Dallas: Center for the Study of Societies in Crisis.

Das, Akhilesh (2010) *Human Rights in Demographic Perspective,* Delhi: Swastik.

De Waal, Alex (1997) *Famine Crimes: Politics and the Disaster Relief Industry in Africa.* London: James Currey and International African Institute.

Dorcey, Tony, with Achim Steiner, Michael Acreman, and Brett Orlando, eds. (1997) *Large Dams: Learning from the Past, Looking at the Future.* Gland, Switzerland: IUCN (the World Conservation Union) and Washington, D.C.: The World Bank.

Duffield, M. And J. Prendergast (1994) *Without Troops and Talks: Humanitarian Intervention in Ethiopia and Eritrea.* Lawrenceville, New Jersey: The Red Sea Press.

Erickson, Laurel (1998) An Assessment of Adjustment Strategies and Satisfaction with Cultural Orientation of Female Refugees: A Qualitative Comparison Between Refugees from Iraq and the Former Soviet Union in a Midwestern American City (Lincoln, Nebraska). M.A. Thesis, University of Nebraska-Lincoln, Lincoln, Nebraska.

Farer, Tom J. (1995) How the International System Copes with Involuntary Migration: Norms, Institutions, and State Practice. *Human Rights Quarterly* 17(1):72-100.

Ferris, E. (1993) *Beyond Borders: Refugees, Migrants, and Human Rights in the Post-Cold War Era.* Trenton, New Jersey: The Red Sea Press and Geneva: the WCC Press.

Giles. W. And H. Moussa, eds. (1996) *Development and Diaspora: Gender and the Refugee Experience*. Dudas, Ontario, Canada: Artemis Publishers.

Gold, Steven (1992) *Refugee Communities*. Newbury Park, California: Sage Publications.

Gordenker, Leon (1987) *Refugees in International Politics*. London and Sydney: Croom Helm.

Gersony, Robert (1989) *Why Somalis Flee: Synthesis of Accounts of Conflict Experience in Northern Somalia by Somali Refugees, Displaced Persons, and Others*. Report to the Bureau for Refugee Programs, Department of State, Washington, D.C.

Gowlland, Vera (1995) *The Problem of Refugees in the Light of Contemporary International Law Issues*. Dordrecht: Martinus Nijhoff.

Hansen, Art and Anthony Oliver-Smith, eds. (1982) *Involuntary Migration and Resettlement: The Problems and Responses of Dislocated People*. Boulder, Colorado: Westview Press.

Hampton, Janie (1998) *Internally Displaced People: A Global Survey*. London: Earthscan Publications.

Hitchcock, Robert K. (2001) *Anthropological Study on the Potential Impact of Refugees in M'Kata, Namibia*. Windhoek, Namibia: United Nations High Commissioner for Refugees.

Hitchcock, Robert K. and Hassan Hussein (1987) Agricultural and Non-Agricultural Settlements for Drought-Afflicted Pastoralists in Somalia. *Disasters* 11(1):30-39.

Holtzman, Jon D. (2000) *Nuer Journeys, Nuer Lives: Sudanese Refugees in Minnesota*. Boston: Allyn and Bacon.

Horowitz, Michael M. (1989) Victims of Development. *Development Anthropology Network* 7(2):1-8.

Horowitz, Michael M. (1991) Victims Upstream and Down. *Journal of Refugee Studies* 4(2):164-181.

Hyndman, Jennifer (2000) *Managing Displacement: Refugees and the Politics of Humanitarianism*. Minneapolis: University of Minnesota Press.

International Organization for Migration (1992) *Migration and the Environment*. Background Paper. Washington, D.C.: The Refugee Policy Group.

International Organization for Migration (1996) *Environmentally-Induced Population Displacements and Environmental Impacts Resulting from Mass Migrations*. Geneva: United Nations High Commissioner for Refugees, the International Organization for Migration, and the Refugee Policy Group.

Jacobson, J. (1988) *Environmental Refugees: A Yardstick of Habitability*. Worldwatch Paper No. 86. Washington, D.C.: WorldWatch Institute.

Jean, Francois, ed. (1992) *Populations in Danger: Medecins San Frontieres*. London: John Libbey and Company.

Kane, Hal (1995) *The Hour of Departure; The Forces that Create Refugees and Migrants*. Worldwatch Paper 125. Washington, D.C.: Worldwatch Institute.

Kibreab, G. (1996) *Ready and Willing . . . But Still Waiting: Eritrean Refugees in Sudan and the Dilemma of Return*. Uppsala, Sweden: Life and Peace Research Institute.

Kibreab, G. (1997) Environmental Causes and Impact of Refugee Movements: A Critique of the Current Debate. *Disasters* 21(1):20-38.

Kleber, Rolf J., Charles R. Figley, and Berthold P.R. Gersons, eds. (1995) *Beyond Trauma: Cultural and Societal Dynamics*. New York and London: Plenum Press.

Koehn, Peter H. (1991) *Refugees from Revolution: U.S. Policy and Third-World Migration*. Boulder, Colorado: Westview Press.

Kourula, Pirkko (1997) *Broadening the Edges: Refugee Definition and International Protection Revisited*. The Hague: Martinus Nijhoff.

Lawson, Michael L. (1994) *Dammed Indians: The Pick Sloan Project and the Missouri River Sioux, 1944-1980*. Second Edition. Norman: University of Oklahoma Press.

Lesotho Highlands Development Authority (1997) Kingdom of Lesotho, Lesotho Highlands Water Project, Compensation Policy. Maseru, Lesotho: Lesotho Highlands Development Authority.

Loescher, Gil (1993) *Beyond Charity: International Cooperation and the Global Refugee Crisis*. Oxford: Oxford University Press.

Macklin, Audrey (1995) Refugee Women and the Imperative of Categories. *Human Rights Quarterly* 17(2):213-277.

Mayotte, J.A. (1992) *Disposable People? The Plight of Refugees*. Maryknoll, New York: Orbis Books.

McCully, Patrick (2001) *Silenced Rivers: The Ecology and Politics of Large Dams*. Second Edition. London and Atlantic Highlands, New Jersey: Zed Books.

McMillan, Della E. (1995) *Sahel Visions: Planned Settlement and River Blindness Control in Burkina Faso*. Tucson: University of Arizona Press.

McMillan, Della E., Thomas Painter, and Thayer Scudder (1992) *Settlement and Development in the River Blindness Control Zone*. World Bank Technical Paper No. 192. Washington, D.C.: World Bank.

McSpadden, Lucia Ann (2000) *Negotiating Return: Conflict and Control in the Repatriation of Eritrean Refugees*. Uppsala, Sweden: Life and Peace Research Institute.

Mollica, Richard F. (1988) The Trauma Story: The Psychiatric

Care of Refugee Survivors of Violence and Torture. In *Post-Traumatic Therapy and Victims of Violence,* Frank M. Ochberg, ed. Pp. 295-314. New York: Brunner/Mazel.

Nicholson, Frances and Patrick Twomey, eds. (1999) *Refugee Rights and Realities: Evolving International Concepts and Regimes.* Cambridge: Cambridge University Press.

Pipher, Mary (2002) *The Middle of Everywhere: The World's Refugees Come to Our Town.* New York and London: Harcourt, Inc.

Rogers, R. And E. Copeland (1993) *Forced Migration: Policy Issues in the Post-Cold War World.* Medford, Massachusetts: The Fletcher School of Law and Diplomacy, Tufts University.

Scudder, Thayer (1962) *The Ecology of the Gwembe Tonga.* Manchester: Manchester University Press for the Rhodes-Livingstone Institute.

Scudder, Thayer (1973) The Human Ecology of Big Projects: River Basin Development and Resettlement. *Annual Review of Anthropology* 4:45-55.

Scudder, Thayer (1980) River-Basin Development and Local Initiative in African Savanna Environments. In *Human Ecology in Savanna Environments,* David Harris, ed. pp. 383-405. New York: Academic Press.

Scudder, Thayer (1981a) What It Means to Be Dammed: The Anthropology of Large-Scale Development Projects in the Tropics and Sub-Tropics. *Engineering and Science* 54(4):9-15.

Scudder, Thayer (1981b) *From Relief to Development: Some Comments on Refugee and Other Settlement in Somalia.* Report to the United States Agency for International Development, Mogadishu, Somalia.

Scudder, Thayer (1989) Conservation Vs. Development: River Basin Projects in Africa. *Environment* 31(2):4-9, 27-32.

Scudder, Thayer (1990) Victims of Development Revisited: The Political Costs of River Basin Development. *IDA Development Anthropology Network* 8(1):1-5.

Scudder, Thayer (1991a) The Need and Justification for Maintaining Trans-Boundary Flood Regimes: The Africa Case. Natural Resources Journal 31(1):75-107.

Scudder, Thayer (1991b) A Sociological Framework for the Analysis of New Lands Settlements. In Putting People First: Sociological Variables in Rural Development (Second Edition), Michael M. Cernea, ed. pp. 148-187. New York: Oxford University Press.

Scudder, Thayer (1993) Development-Induced Relocation and Refugee Studies: 37 Years of Change and Continuity among Zambia's Gwembe Tonga. *Journal of Refugee Studies* 6(2):123-152.

Scudder, Thayer (1997a) Social Impacts. In *Water Resources: Environmental Planning, Management, and Development,* Asit K. Biswas, ed. pp. 623-665. London: Macmillan.

Scudder, Thayer (1997b) Resettlement. In *Water Resources: Environmental Planning, Management, and Development,* Asit K. Biswas, ed. Pp. 667-710. London: Macmillan.

Scudder, Thayer and Elizabeth Colson (1979) Long-term Research in the Gwembe Valley, Zambia. In *Long-term Field Research in Social Anthropology,* George Forster, Thayer Scudder, Elizabeth Colson, and Robert V. Kemper, eds. Pp. 227-254. New York, Academic Press.

Seymour, Frances J. And Vir Singh (1995) *A Preliminary Review of Experience with Resettlement to Achieve Conservation Objectives.* Washington, D.C.: World Wildlife Fund.

Smyser, W.R. (1987) *Refugees: Extended Exile.* New York and Westport, Connecticut: Praeger and Washington, D.C.: The Center for Strategic and International Studies.

Spooner, Bryan (1984) *Refugee Settlement in the Lower Shabelle Region, Somalia.* Report to the National Refugee Commission and Save the Children Federation, (USA), Mogadishu, Somalia.

United Nations High Commissioner for Refugees (1993) *The State of the World's Refugees: The Challenge of Protection.* Oxford: Oxford University Press.

United Nations High Commissioner for Refugees (1995) *The State of the World's Refugees: In Search of Solutions.* Oxford: Oxford University Press.

United Nations High Commissioner for Refugees (1998) *The State of the World's Refugees: A Humanitarian Agenda.* Oxford: Oxford University Press.

United States Committee for Refugees (1995) *World Refugee Survey.* Washington, D.C.: Immigration and Refugee Services of America.

United States Committee for Refugees (1997) *World Refugee Survey.* Washington, D.C.: Immigration and Refugee Services of America.

United Nations Development Program (2000) *Human Rights and Human Development: 2000 Human Development Program.* New York: United Nations.

Van der Veer, Guus (1998) *Counseling and Therapy with Refugees and Victims of Trauma: Psychological Problems of Victims of War, Torture, and Repression.* Second Edition. Chichester and New York: John Wiley and Sons.

Warner, Daniel, ed. (1995) *New Dimensions of Peacekeeping..* Dordrecht: Martinus Nijhoff.

Weiner, Myron (1995) *The Global Migration Crisis: Challenge to States and to Human Rights*. New York: Addison-Wesley Longman Publishers.

Wilks, Alex and Nicholas Hildyard (1994) Evicted! The World Bank and Forced Resettlement. *The Ecologist* 24(6):225-229.

Willis, Mary (2002) The Nuer and the Dinka Take Refuge in Nebraska: The Cattle Are Lowing But It's Not the Sudan. Paper presented at the 62nd annual meetings of the Society for Applied Anthropology, Atlanta, Georgia, March 6-10, 2002.

Wishart, David J. (1990) *Compensation for Dispossession: Payments to the Indians for Their Land on the Central and Northern Great Plains in the 19th Century*. National Geographic Research 6(1):94-109.

Wood, William B. (1994) Forced Migration: Local Conflicts and International Dilemmas. *Annals of the Association of American Geographers* 84(4):607-634.

World Bank (1990) Operational Directive 4.30: Involuntary Resettlement. *World Bank Operational Manual*. Washington, D.C.: World Bank.

World Bank (1991a) *Environmental Assessment Sourcebook 1991*. Washington, D.C: The World Bank.

World Bank (1991b) Operational Directive 4.20: Indigenous Peoples. *The World Bank Operational Manual*. Washington, D.C.: The World Bank.

World Bank (1992) *World Development Report 1992: Development and the Environment*. Washington, D.C.: The World Bank.

World Bank (1993a) *Early Experience with Involuntary Resettlement: Impact Evaluation on Thailand Khao Laem Hydroelectric (Loan 1770-TH)*. Operations Evaluation Department, World Bank, 29 June, 1993.

World Bank (1993b) *Early Experience in Involuntary Resettlement: Overview*. Report No. 12142, June 1993. Washington, D.C.: World Bank.

World Bank (1994a) *Resettlement and Development: The Bankwide Review Projects Involving Involuntary Resettlement, 1986-1993*. Washington, D.C.: World Bank.

World Bank (1996) *The World Bank's Experience with Large Dams: A Preliminary Review of Impacts*. Washington, D.C.: Operations Evaluation Department, World Bank.

World Health Organization (1996) *Mental Health of Refugees*. Geneva: World Health Organization (WHO).

# Glossary

**Application registration card (ARC):** ARC is a credit card sized document issued to asylum applicants after screening to show that they have applied for asylum. It is also used as evidence of identity, immigration status and entitlements in the UK. It holds identifying information including fingerprints and reporting arrangements in a microchip within the card.

**Asylum interview:** An asylum interview is a substantive interview about a person's reasons for claiming asylum in the UK.

**Asylum Screening Unit:** Asylum screening units are the entry points into the asylum system. It is here that in-country asylum seekers make their initial asylum claims and where immigration officers conduct screening interviews.

**Asylum seeker:** An asylum seeker is someone who has lodged an application for protection on the basis of the Refugee Convention or Article 3 of the ECHR.

**Asylum support:** Asylum seekers who are destitute may be able to receive accommodation and/or subsistence support from the UK Border Agency (UKBA). This form of support is also referred to as 'UKBA support', see below. If they have additional care needs, due to chronic illness or disability they may also be eligible to support from their local authority.

**Asylum Support Adjudicators:** Asylum Support Adjudicators consider appeals by asylum seekers against UKBA decisions to refuse or terminate asylum support.

**Asylum Support Partnership (ASP):** The Asylum Support Partnership comprises of Refugee Action, Refugee Council, Scottish Refugee Council and Welsh Refugee Council which are contracted by UKBA to provide advice and support to asylum seekers and refugees. The Asylum Support Partnership used to be called the Inter Agency Partnership.

**Case resolution process:** The case resolution process was set up by the UKBA to deal with unresolved cases of those who claimed asylum before April 2007. Claims are being dealt with by the Case Resolution Directorate at the UK Border Agency. It is expected that case resolution will take until 2011 to complete.

**Certificate of Travel:** Certificate of Travel, also known as the 'Home Office travel document' can be issued to people who have humanitarian protection or discretionary leave. The Certificate of Travel is not valid to travel to the country of origin.

**Clearly unfounded claims:** When the UKBA believes that the asylum seeker comes from a safe country and would not face a risk of being persecuted, it deems it a 'clearly unfounded case'.

**Convention Travel Document (CTD):** A Convention Travel Document, also known as 'blue document' is given to people with refugee status to use as a valid travel document in place of passport to travel overseas. This document is valid for all countries except the one from which the person sought asylum.

**Discretionary leave:** Discretionary leave is a form of immigration status granted to a person who the Home Office has decided does not qualify for refugee status or humanitarian protection but where there are other strong reasons why the person needs to stay in the UK temporarily.

**Dublin II Regulation:** Dublin II Regulation provides EU member states with a mechanism for allocating responsibility to a single member state for processing an asylum claim.

**European Convention on Human Rights (ECHR):** The ECHR is an international legal instrument adopted under the auspices of the Council of Europe. Its provisions are enforceable in UK law courts.

**Explore and Prepare:** 'Explore and Prepare' is a Government funded programme which allows a group of refugees to visit their country of origin to assess the situation and prepare for their permanent return.

**Family reunion:** Family reunion is the policy enabling people bring their spouse and dependent children join them in the UK.

**HC1 form:** Application form for help with medical costs.

**HC2 certificate:** Certificate which allows someone to claim free prescriptions and some dental and optical services.

**Human Rights Act 1998:** The Human Rights Act incorporated the European Convention on Human Rights (ECHR) into the UK law.

**Humanitarian protection (HP):** Humanitarian protection is a form of immigration status. It is granted by the Home Office to a person who it decides has a need for protection but who does not meet the criteria for refugee status.

**Immigration judge:** An immigration judge is a person appointed by the Lord Chancellor to decide appeals made to the Asylum and Immigration Tribunal.

**Immigration removal centre:** Immigration removal centres are detention centres. They are used to detain people under Immigration Act powers, including those at any stage of the asylum process, not as the title might imply, just prior to removal.

**Immigration service:** The Immigration Service is the UKBA department that regulates entry at UK ports, screens asylum seekers, manages asylum cases and contact with asylum seekers, and enforces removal of people who don't have permission to remain in the country.

**Indefinite leave to remain (ILR):** ILR is a form of immigration status given by the UK Border Agency. Indefinite leave to remain (ILR) is also called 'permanent residence' or 'settled status' as it gives permission to stay in the UK on a permanent basis.

**Integration loans:** Integration loans are available to people who have been granted refugee status or humanitarian protection.

**Legal representative:** Legal representative is a barrister or a solicitor, solicitor's employee or other authorised person who acts for an applicant or appellant in relation to a claim.

**NASS 35:** A NASS 35 is a UKBA document which states that the holder is no longer entitled to support as they have received a positive decision on their asylum application. It is used to demonstrate that they are eligible for welfare benefits.

**Naturalisation:** Naturalisation is the process of becoming a British national.

**New Asylum Model (NAM):** The New Asylum Model was introduced by the UKBA for all new asylum claims in April 2007. NAM entails a 'case owner' from the UKBA who is responsible for processing the application from beginning to end.

**Non-suspensive appeals (NSA):** When a claim for asylum falls under the non-suspensive appeals process it means that the applicant only has the right to appeal against a negative UKBA decision once outside of the UK.

**Office of the Immigration Services Commissioner:** The Commissioner regulates immigration advice in the UK.

**One stop appeal:** The one stop appeal procedure aims to ensure that all grounds for appeal are dealt at one appeal only.

**One Stop Service:** One Stop Services are provided by the Asylum Support Partnership under contract with the UKBA. See 'Asylum Support Partnership'.

**Overstayer:** An overstayer is a person who was allowed into the UK for a limited period but who has remained longer than the time allowed without permission from the Home Office or under the immigration rules.

**Port applicant:** A person who applies for asylum to the immigration officer at an airport or seaport when she/he first arrives, ie. before passing through immigration control.

**Refugee:** A refugee is a person who 'owing to a well-founded fear of being persecuted for reasons of race, religion, nationality, membership of a particular social group, or political opinion, is outside the country of his nationality, and is unable to or, owing to such fear, is unwilling to avail himself of the protection of that country...' (Definition quoted from the 1951 Refugee Convention)

**Refugee Convention:** Refugee Convention means the United Nations Convention Relating to the Status of Refugees 1951 and the 1967 Protocol.

**Refugee status:** Refugee status is awarded to someone the UKBA recognises as a refugee as described in the Refugee Convention.

**Removal:** Removal is a process whereby immigration officers enforce return from the UK to another country.

**Reporting:** Most asylum seekers who are not detained are expected to report to a reporting centre or police station.

**Resettlement:** Resettlement if the process whereby refugees living outside their country of origin are moved to another country for permanent resettlement. See 'Gateway Protection Programme'.

**Separated children:** Separated children are children under 18 years of age who are outside their country of origin and separated from both parents, or previous/legal customary care giver. Separated children are typically asylum seekers, but not in every case.

**Standard acknowledgement letter (SAL):** In some cases, the UKBA will not be able to issue an asylum registration card, see Application registration card. Instead, a standard acknowledgement letter may be given which acknowledges an asylum application.

**Statement of evidence form (SEF):** A UKBA form which separated children applying for asylum use to set out their grounds for claiming asylum. The form was previously used for all asylum seekers.

**Voluntary Assisted Return & Reintegration Programme (VAARP):** Voluntary Assisted Return & Reintegration Programme is a UK scheme to help people return permanently to their home country. The scheme is operated by the International Organization for Migration for the UK Border Agency. See 'International Organization for Migration'.

# INDEX